SHRINK
GOVERNMENT:
IT'S TOO
BIG!

SHRINK GOVERNMENT:
IT'S TOO
BIG!

Archie Richards

DEFIANCE PRESS
& PUBLISHING

Shrink Governmment: It's Too Big!

DEFIANCE PRESS
& PUBLISHING

ISBN-13: 978-1-959677-98-7 (Paperback)
ISBN-13: 978-1-959677-97-0 (eBook)

Author's photo by Katie Baca of Concord, NH

Published by Defiance Press and Publishing, LLC

Bulk orders of this book may be obtained by contacting Defiance Press and Publishing, LLC at: www.defiancepress.com.

Public Relations Dept. – Defiance Press & Publishing, LLC
281-581-9300
pr@defiancepress.com

Defiance Press & Publishing, LLC
281-581-9300
info@defiancepress.com

DEDICATION

To those who suffer from the excessive reach and power of government.

Acknowledgements

I appreciate the computer assistance of Jesse Dorland and Kyle Stockbridge.

Thanks to Andy Subbiondo for his advice about the title.

TABLE OF CONTENTS

FOREWORD

I HAVE MANAGED TO DEVELOP two professional skills. Writing is one. The other is the performance of classical concert piano. Before Covid, I was engaged in both, writing books that were published by Defiance Press & Publishing, writing columns every couple of weeks for friends and the Concord Monitor, and also playing concerts and singalongs for retirement homes and senior centers mostly in Boston area. After the lockdowns were imposed, my musical performances came to a halt. What to do with the time? *Ah-ha, I'll turn the columns into a book.*

I had accumulated voluminous files to back up my previous books. I did not accumulate more backups for this book. I just plowed ahead, usually obtaining information, when necessary, from the Web. But after I presented the book to the publisher, the editor pointed out, correctly, that I needed to cite references.

Which leads me to apologize to you, dear reader. Most of the written material I had in my files are dated from 2019 to 2022. They're not wrong. They still serve to back up the numerous generalities I present in this book. They're just not current. But life in America in the last year or two has become worse, not better. If my backup materials were more current, they would probably support my generalities all the more.

INTRODUCTION

DO YOU SUSPECT AMERICA IS going wrong and are not sure why? This is the right book for you.

Not only are the policies of American governments wrong, there are too many of them, too many laws, too many regulations, too much use of force. In combination, they do more harm than good.

Only the people who work for government are permitted to exercise force. They are doing it altogether too much. The bigger the government, the more force is applied, and the more dysfunctional the nation becomes. In the long run, society is most content when force is held to a minimum.

The U.S. Constitution spells out specific policies the federal government is permitted to enact, and no others. But big-government people have latched onto two words in the Constitution, "general welfare." Those two words, they figure, give them the right to do anything they darn well please. If the words were removed from the Constitution, most of what the multi-headed monster is doing would probably become unconstitutional.

Big government and high tax rates enable more and more wealth to flow through government. The unintended result, explained below, is that the rich become richer and the gap between rich and poor becomes wider. Time and again, the actual, long-run results of big-government policies are the opposite of the intended results.

Our federal, state, and local governments now constitute about

40 percent of the Gross Domestic Product (GDP). This is far too large a share. The combination of millions of requirements embodied in the multitude of laws and regulations spells big trouble.

The world's first constitution was written by none other than John Adams for the Commonwealth of Massachusetts. It seemed natural for eighteenth century Americans to adopt a constitution. As farmers, most of them were the sole owners of their own businesses. They took responsibility for themselves and wanted little government interference.

Current Americans may own stocks, representing tiny portions of companies, but few of them are sole business owners. Most current Americans, in fact, expect much from government. This causes all sorts of problems.

Here's the damaging sequence America has undertaken for over a century: Government solutions result in bigger government and more use of force. These cause problems in addition to the ones the government first dealt with. Government then designs solutions for the new problems. The new solutions create even more problems. The result: a massive government and a multitude of problems, hurting the poor most.

Liberals assume that the supply of other peoples' money is inexhaustible. But the growth of government quenches the creation of wealth and makes other peoples' money less available. In the long run, government thus creates ever more needs, but suppresses the availability of money to deal with them. America's current dysfunction would suggest that the long run has come home to roost.

Government consumes wealth, creates no wealth, and inhibits the creation of wealth. If it were greatly diminished, the income of most people would rise, and the gap between rich and poor would narrow. You'll find considerable evidence in this book.

It is time to place individual liberty at the forefront of our lives.

Visit ArchieRichards.com to help get this book into as many hands as possible, with the goal of influencing public policies for the better.

CHAPTER 1

CORPORATE MANAGERS

UNFORTUNATELY, CURRENT MANAGERS OF BIG American companies are actively seeking government's help in crowding out their smaller competitors. They may expect that they and top government officials will walk arm in arm toward ever greater powers and profits.

The managers may be in for a surprise. America is closer to a totalitarian government than most people think. Dictators dislike prominent and talented people who disagree with them. The managers of big American corporations may find themselves disappearing from the earth.

Naah. Can't happen. The Constitution won't allow it.

Dream on, friend, dream on.

ARMED TO THE TEETH

In 1832, John Marshall, Chief Justice of the U.S. Supreme Court, rendered a judicial opinion with which President Andrew Jackson disagreed. Jackson was reported to have said, "John Marshall has made his decision. Now let him enforce it."

A future Supreme Court may decide that various policies of the federal government, such as those described in this book, are unconstitutional. The federal bureaucracy already seems to be taking measures that would prevent those decisions from being enforced. Here's evidence:

The February 20, 2019, issue of *Newsmax* cited a report from the U.S. Government Accountability Office saying that, from 2010 to 2017, twenty non-military "law enforcement" agencies spent at least $38.8 million on firearms, $325.9 million on ammunition, and $1.14 billion on tactical equipment.

By 2017, the IRS had 4,487 guns, including 15 fully automatic machine guns and 5.1 million rounds of ammunition. (Everyone knows that machine guns are essential when you're auditing taxpayers.)

The Health and Human Services Office of the Inspector General had 194 fully automatic firearms and 386,952 rounds of ammo. (Inspector-Generalship is always hazardous.)

The EPA had 377 pistols with 220,418 pistol rounds and 223 shot-guns with 146,975 shotgun rounds. (Those dirty polluters, you gotta watch 'em every minute.)

The FDA had 390 pistols with 166,783 pistol rounds and 122 shot-guns with 30,620 shotgun rounds. (You'd be a fool to inspect meat or research drugs without being armed.)

(The deplorables may attack us at any time, probably with the Supreme Court's support. They must not succeed. What does the Court know about administrative government anyway?)

CHAPTER 2

HOW TO RESOLVE THE DEBT CRISIS
WITH MINIMUM STRESS

AMERICA IS HEADED FOR A crackup. At $33 trillion, the national debt is considerably higher than the GDP of $23 trillion. The debt is growing faster than the economy. It's likely that the government must borrow just to pay the interest. After interest rates return to their normal, higher levels, the cost of carrying the federal debt will crowd out current expenses. Future Americans, who did not incur *our* debt, will refuse to pay it off and will vote out of office legislators who insist on raising taxes to do so. There's darkness at the end of the tunnel, and the tunnel isn't all that long.

But there's a way out. The federal government owns 28 percent of the nation's land and several billion dollars' worth of gold. Those assets should be transferred to private parties in return for the new owners accepting portions of the nation's debts. The debt would no longer be owed by the federal government, where it probably can't be repaid. It would be owed by the owners of productive resources, where it can.

Other than the gold, the productive resources include farmland, forests, prairies, swamps, deserts, hills, mountains, valleys, rivers, waterways, aquifers, land below the surface, reservoirs, roads, interstates, bridges, dams, the national parks, and the twelve-mile band of ocean that rings the nation.

What? The national parks!

Why not? With few exceptions, government is the worst and most expensive way to manage anything. If the owners of national parks cause the long-term values to deteriorate in favor of short-term profits, the people and the media would call in no uncertain terms for reversals.

Amtrak, urban transportation, and the postal service should be owned and operated by private parties. The 600,000 people employed by the U.S. Postal Service are the highest paid unskilled workers in the world. There may be a potential for cost-saving there. Too many urban buses are driven around almost empty, spewing exhaust, and losing money. Thousands of self-employed car-owners would stand ready to provide rides for modest fees. Women given such rides would be safe if they carry weapons and know how to use them.

The individuals and corporations that own portions of the Mississippi River could charge people and businesses that use the waters for irrigation, drinking, transportation, manufacturing, fishing, and recreation. After Congress limits the liability of the owners for floods, the value of the river would be sky-high, enabling the owners to take on considerable federal debt.

The resources would have a variety of owners. One might make available a mountain she owns for low-cost hiking. Another might plan the construction of a mine.

Private parties would also own the nation's roads. The roads should be embedded with electronic devices that could identify the vehicles using the road, their weight, the time of day, and possibly the road's condition. All vehicles would have equivalent devices. The road owners would charge the vehicle owners regularly, with the prices higher during commuting hours and possibly when the roads are covered with ice or snow. Roads used infrequently would probably be freebies.

Truckers would be fully charged for their wear and tear of the roads, which they are not now. The higher charges would likely suppress long-distance trucking, which is expensive, and stimulate rail and water transportation, which are less so.

With state and local tax rates cut, the public's cost of transportation would be reduced significantly.

Some of the private parties taking ownership of portions of the national debt would end up unable to pay their debts. But the nation would be better off transferring the assets to private parties anyway because corrective measures are far more likely to be found by the private sector than if the government continued to own the debt.

Okay, but what's to keep the government debt from rebuilding? This is crucial.

Answer: The members of Congress must serve for one term only. Never standing for reelection, they would have far less incentive to vote for government benefits for constituents. Of the many recommendations in this book, this is the most important. After the two-year term, members of the House must leave. While we're at it, senatorial terms should be reduced to four years. Presidents must leave for good after four years; Supreme Court judges, ten years. Constitutional amendments would be required, of course. An amendment that prevents new members of Congress from standing for reelection might pass if current members, to a certain extent, are grandfathered in.

Some would say that requiring legislators to leave office so soon would interfere with their trying new ideas and learning the ways of government. Nonsense. The government has implemented too many new ideas that caused more harm than good. Legislators don't need to learn the ways of government. They should instead reverse the myriad of policies that are doing harm and make government much smaller. Presidential elections would be less of a circus because less would be at stake. People accustomed to receiving help from the government would learn ever more about the possibilities of the private sector.

The compensation of federal legislators should be cut from current levels, and their compensation should be cut even more after a federal deficit is incurred. We would want people to run for office, not to exercise power or become wealthy, but because it's their turn to serve.

After the federal government sells the resources it owns in return for private parties assuming the debt, some of the debt might be left over, unsold. But if the government sector is greatly reduced, with legislators limited to a single term and income-tax rates sharply cut, the government would have a significant surplus, which could be used to pay off the remaining federal debt. Tax rates could then be lowered even more.

When tax rates are high and taxpayers are uncomfortable paying what they owe, lowering the rates causes the economy to grow and the government revenues to increase, as explained later in this book. But when tax rates are already low and flat, and taxpayers are comfortable paying what they owe, lowering the rates would probably cause the revenues to fall. If the people are pleased with a modest government, it is possible that taxation could eventually be abolished, and all government revenues would be voluntary gifts. For this, I'm not holding my breath.

What about support for people whose needs are not sufficiently met by the private sector? As discussed below, individuals and associations would raise money from the prosperous and provide it to those who are suffering, often with conditions. Even now, high-income people accept sky-high tax rates. With the rates greatly reduced, they would want to help.

The debt crisis cannot be resolved without political and personal stress. Can you think of a realistic way to resolve the issue with less stress than this?

CHAPTER 3

WELFARE THAT DOESN'T CREATE POVERTY

NUMEROUS TELEVISION STORIES HAVE PORTRAYED rich people as bad guys. If the government vacated the welfare business and significantly reduced income-tax rates, most rich people would fail to step forward to help the poor, right?

Turn off the tube. Most employers do care about their employees and to some extent about society at large. The more government is reduced, the more employers would care about their employees and about society at large. With tax rates low, prosperous people would provide ample help themselves or pay others to do it.

Around 1900, when government was much smaller, charity directories in the big cities took as many as one hundred pages to describe voluntary agencies that dealt with every imaginable emergency. If government were reduced now, non-government welfare agencies would again spring to life. The media might assist, promulgating messages such as, "Mr. Big Bucks of this community has displayed his wealth by building a huge home and buying a stupendous yacht. But he has given little to alleviate poverty." This would enliven the gentleman's charitable impulses.

In effect, the government has said, "We'll take care of helping others. You need only provide the funds." Some wealthy individuals have taken this seriously and not bothered to help others. But if government were cut way back and prevented from engaging in the helping business, the wealthy, especially with tax rates reduced, would spring into action, just as they did 125 years ago.

A study by Harvard social scientists found that people with low income who receive significant government handouts increase their spending, work less, feel worse about their work, and feel worse about themselves. A different study found that people with low income who received food stamps subsequently ate less-healthy food than those who didn't. Those cherished liberal programs are so helpful, aren't they?

With welfare so often paid to single mothers, millions of black children have no father living in the home, creating huge problems for those children and for the entire society. Boys who grow up without fathers are more likely to fail in school and display violent behavior. A non-government person from the private sector who administers the payments for support could council the mother to find a man who's willing to commit to the family and maybe council the man about how to achieve marital happiness. The administrator should have the discretion to impose work requirements, adjust the amount of the payments, and provide welfare payments to both. The payments would not be so large as to keep the individual from looking for work. Government welfare workers are given no such discretion. All welfare payments go to the woman with little or no counseling.

People in the public sector, afraid of being blamed for individual initiative, are likely to just go along and toe the line. People in the private sector are far more likely to exercise individual initiative.

Welfare was originally intended to be temporary help for people down on their luck. But over time, it has transformed into a massive entitlement that breeds dependence on government – just what liberals want. Voters should move welfare to the private sector and get government out of the way. With income tax rates much reduced, ample money would become available.

There was considerable poverty in America in the nineteenth and early twentieth centuries, but the poorest people tended to be new immigrants. People who had been here a while took care of themselves or were reasonably well cared for by private-sector welfare. Americans were highly optimistic, and the poor rose quickly into the middle class.

The entrepreneurs who created new technologies in the nineteenth century became fabulously wealthy, but not at the expense of other Americans, as liberals proclaim. Their developments raised *everyone's* standard of living. Researchers have found that the cost of living for the very rich rose rapidly due to the increase in wages of the people who supplied their goods and services. The wages of their servants also rose rapidly. The cost of living of the rich thus fell more slowly than it did for everyone else.

Market entrepreneurs benefited everyone, as mentioned. But political entrepreneurs, who catered to politicians, benefited mostly themselves. These included railroad magnates who became rich from government subsidies, manufacturers who profited from tariffs, and state bankers who were protected from out-of-state competitors.[1]

Today's large, inflexible government welfare payments cause too many people to remain at the lowest income level. If the government were cut back and free-market capitalism prevailed, the poor would gain wealth faster than the rich. As a group, they wouldn't catch up to the rich, of course, because people have different capabilities, inclinations, earning power, and cultural traditions. But the people occupying the lowest income rung would change more frequently than they do now. The occupants of all income levels, in fact, would change more frequently.

Monarchies freeze social mobility. If the monarch, dukes, duchesses, and other medieval titles in the United Kingdom were done away with, the opportunities for people in the lower classes to reach the top would greatly increase.

---

1. Vincent Geloso, "Actually, the Gilded Age was Awesome for Equality." American Institute for Economic Research (AIER), October 25, 2019.

Income from a job increases a person's morale. Income from welfare reduces it. It's time to shrink government and let the private sector handle welfare. It would do the job more effectively than government. The feeling that we're all in this together, even for a nation as large as the United States, would take hold, and the underclass would flourish.

CHAPTER 4

GLOBAL WARMING: A BOGUS ISSUE

EVIDENTLY THE U.S. GOVERNMENT WANT us to think that the world temperature has never been higher. Wrong. The "Roman Climatic Optimum" had unusually warm weather from approximately 250 BC to AD 400, helping to bring the Roman Empire to its apex. Since the ocean was one or two meters higher than it is now, the boats of old could readily sail up the Tiber River to Rome's harbor. The earth has since become colder and the ocean level has fallen, making the harbor far less accessible.

Around the year AD 1000 the Vikings landed on a heavily forested island they named "Greenland." The glaciers had largely melted. The world was warmer than it is now, although not as warm as it was during the Roman Climatic Optimum.

A search for "Ocean levels Manhattan 1856 to the Present" brings up the following chart.

RELATIVE SEA LEVEL TREND
8518750 THE BATTERY, NEW YORK

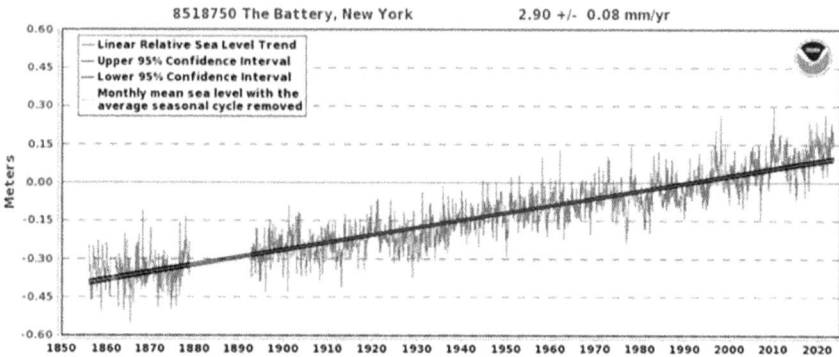

Credit: Graph from NOAA Tides & CURRENTS. https://tidesandcurrents.noaa.gov/sltrends/
sltrends_station.shtml?id=8518750

Starting around the time of World War II, industrial emissions of carbon dioxide (CO2) became significant. Yet you may note from the above website that the ocean rose no faster after World War II than it did before. The levels of CO2, in fact, have nothing to do with temperatures. Variations in global temperatures do not correlate with changes in atmospheric CO2. They correlate with solar activity, atmospheric cycles, and cycles of ocean currents.

With significant fluctuations, the world temperature has been rising since the end of the last ice age, 12,000 years ago. In recent decades, the percentages of CO2 and nitrogen (also a byproduct of fossil fuel combustion) have risen modestly in the atmosphere. The result has been highly beneficial. Since 1982, green foliage has expanded throughout the world by an area twice size of the continental U.S. The U.S. frost-free growing season has increased by two weeks since 1970.[2]

To measure atmospheric temperatures, the National Oceanic and Atmospheric Administration (NOAA) set up about 1,000 stations in the U.S., specifying that the instruments be placed "over level earth or sod ter-

2. Marlo Lewis, Jr. "A Citizen's Guide to Climate Change," Competitive Enterprise Institute, June 11, 2019.

rain typical of the area around the station and at least one hundred feet from any extensive concrete or paved surface." These are sensible conditions, but NOAA has not complied with them. After an extensive study, the Heartland Institute reported that 96 percent of the stations were too close to asphalt, cement, machinery, and other heat-trapping objects. The data from the 4 percent of the stations that did comply with the standards showed rates of warming almost half that of all the stations.[3]

NOAA originally measured ocean temperatures from buoys, which made sense. But NOAA discarded the buoys and began recording the water temperatures in ship ballasts. Big ships are made of metal, which absorbs heat from the sun. The water in their ballasts is therefore warmer than that of the surrounding ocean. This enabled the government to exaggerate the warming.

About two-thirds of the earth is typically covered with clouds, reflecting massive amounts of heat into space. The computer models used by proponents of global warming assume that the skies are cloudless 24-7 throughout the world. Poof! The models show cataclysmic warming. *That was easy. With fraudulent models like that, we can scare the public half to death.*

Neither the temperature nor the ocean level has risen anywhere near as fast as the government wants us to believe. Why the deception? Because the government seeks control of many aspects of our lives: what we drive, what we eat, the temperatures of our homes and buildings, how much electricity we use. Citizens won't allow such control unless they believe the consequences of not doing so would be severe.

National Geographic Magazine has shown drawings of New York City with several floors of skyscrapers flooded by ocean waters, supposedly due to global warming. Those drawings are nonsense. There is, however, a danger of the New York subway system being flooded, although not from

---

3. Heartland Institute, "New Surface Stations Report Released – It's Worse That We Thought," July 27, 2022.

global warming: The volcanic Azore Islands, off the coast of Portugal, experience constant earthquakes. Corvo and Flores, the western-most islands, have steep cliffs along the ocean, facing west. If one of them suffers a major earthquake, enormous amounts of earth and rocks could fall into the ocean, possibly causing a tsunami. This could affect New York City significantly since the entrance to the harbor would funnel the tsunami and make it higher. All of this is unlikely, but it's possible. It is more likely, however, than global warming causing worldwide flooding. That's not likely at all.

Other than Manhattan, there are few places where the sea level has been recorded for long periods. A search for "Ocean Levels, Newlyn, UK 1915 to the Present" brings up the following chart. Why the chart ends at 2014 I do not know.

NEWLYN MONTHLY MEAN SEA LEVEL

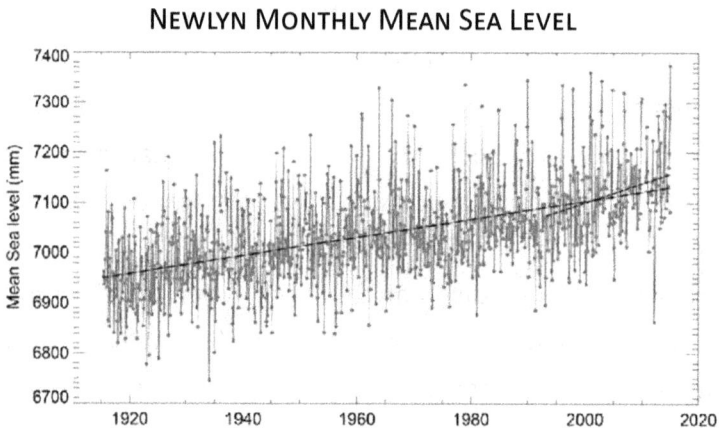

Credit: https://www.researchgate.net/publication/298795816_A_Century_of_Sea_Level_Measurements_at_Newlyn_Southwest_England   page 126

The lengthy explanation accompanying this chart says that the average rate of change of the mean sea level for the last 60 years was 1.8 mm/year. But during the years 1993-2014, illustrated by the short black line angling upward, the average rate of change was 3.8 mm/year.

Let's assume the faster rate, 3.8 millimeters a year. Multiplying this by 100 results in 380 millimeters in 100 years. To convert to meters, divide 380 millimeters by 1,000. The result is 0.38 meters, meaning that the increase in sea level in 100 years would be a little over one-third of a meter. This would mean a rise in the ocean level of a little more than a meter in 300 years. That's a lot, but it's considerably less than the multi-meter rise projected by global-warming proponents. Their purpose is to scare us out of our wits.

A year ago, a chart was available on the Internet showing the ocean level measured in China for about the last 60 years. That chart seems to have been removed.

Some scientists maintain that, when atmospheric CO2 increases, warming becomes inevitable. Well, the largest *percentage* increase in man-caused atmospheric CO2 lasted from 1938 to about 1980. Yet during this 42-year period, temperatures did not rise; they fell. This provides all the more evidence that atmospheric CO2 has no effect on temperatures.

Global-warming proponents are striving to make the earth colder. Cold kills about 20 times as many people as heat.[4] The prosperous proponents, nicely bundled up in well-insulated homes, might not care.

The U.S. government wants us to believe that the summer of 2023 was the warmest ever. Not so. Several previous summers were hotter, especially in the 1930s. Besides, a reasonable amount of warming would benefit living things.

Most people would be surprised to learn that CO2 is a minute percentage of the atmosphere: 430 parts per million. CO2 is just a single part out of 2,326 atmospheric parts (one million divided by 430), and some of that tiny portion fuels the earth's plant life. Yet global-warming proponents expect that what's left of the CO2 after supplying the earth's plant life would cause cataclysmic warming. This seems highly unlikely. Anyway, the earth's most important source of energy is not CO2; it's the sun.

Even with the increases of atmospheric CO2 caused by industrial-

4. Marlo Lewis, Jr. "A Citizen's Guide to Climate Change," Competitive Enterprise Institute, June 11, 2019.

ization, the current concentration is lower than it has been during 95 percent of the earth's history.

Renewable energy from sunlight and wind is far less concentrated than that of fossil fuels. Renewables require more land, rare earths, and other inputs than fossil fuels. Since the sun doesn't shine and the wind doesn't blow all the time, renewables require fossil-fuel backups. But these can't be turned on and off like light switches; they must be run continually, which helps to make renewables prohibitively expensive.

A *Wall Street Journal* column, "In Defense of Carbon Dioxide," which this author retained, was published on May 8, 2013. One author, Harrison H. Schmitt, had been a geologist, astronaut walker on the moon, and a U.S. Senator from New Mexico. At the time of the column, he was an adjunct professor of engineering at the University of Wisconsin. The other author, William Happer, had been Director of the Office of Energy Research at the U.S. Department of Energy. When the column was written, he was a professor of physics at Princeton.

The authors decry the government's designation of carbon dioxide as a dangerous pollutant. It is anything but. Operators of commercial greenhouses increase the levels of carbon dioxide from the current 430 parts per million to 1,000 ppm or more to improve the growth and quality of their plants.

The authors further explain that wheat, rice, soybeans, cotton, and many forage crops evolved when the percentage of CO_2 in the atmosphere was more like 3,000 parts per million, not the current 430. The crops are currently undernourished. To compensate, the plants developed tiny holes in their leaves, called "stomata." The holes enable moisture to enter the leaf from which CO_2 is drawn. But this process requires far more chemical energy than simply absorbing CO_2 from the air.

With 8 billion people to feed, the world needs more CO_2, not less. If CO_2 were more like 3000 parts per million, life would flourish on land and sea.

Bjorn Lomborg, founder of the think tank, Copenhagen Consensus Center, has written and broadcast extensively about global warming. Lomborg plugged data from the U.S. Inflation Reduction Act of 2022 into the United Nations warming models and calculated that the world temperature in 2100, almost 8 decades from now, would fall a *maximum* of 0.028° Fahrenheit. (That's 28 thousandths of one degree.) Daily fluctuations of temperatures are considerably greater than 0.028°. If you wanted to reduce the temperature of a room by 0.028°, from 72° to 71.972°F, you probably couldn't control the thermostat dial precisely enough to register so small a change.

The government purports to control the weather. Yeah sure. Its real objective is to control our lives.

In September 2022, the *Epoch Times* interviewed Patrick Moore, who co-founded Greenpeace in 1971. He left Greenpeace 15 years later because it was no longer concerned with the science of atmospheric temperatures. Greenpeace's 2,000 employees focused on instilling fear and guilt, encouraging the public to send them money. Its campaigns against fossil fuels, nuclear energy, and CO2 were designed to make people think civilization will come to an end unless the economy is crippled.[5]

Global warming is a bogus issue. The world needs more CO2, not less.

ANOTHER BOGUS ISSUE: RACISM

Are you racist?

You may not know for sure. I don't. If people were polled nationwide, the responses would be unreliable. But observing how people spend their money is quite another matter. American whites watch numerous

5. The same information was published by Climate Depot, a project of CFACT, on September 8, 2022. That publication adds that, whereas Greenpeace and many politicians say that polar bears are going extinct because of the lack of Arctic ice, the truth is, the polar bear population has grown from 6,000-to-8,000 in 1973 to 30,000-to-50,000 today.

television advertisements that prominently feature blacks. If the whites were racist, watching such ads would make them uncomfortable, and they wouldn't buy the products being advertised. Another indicator of the degree of racism: How much do people spend on tickets for movies whose leading characters are black?

Back in the 1950s, when America truly was racist, advertisements seldom included blacks because the ad designers knew those wouldn't work. The most prominent black in ads was the non-threatening Aunt Jemima, and she wasn't a real person. In movies, blacks appeared mostly as servants.

In 1958, Gallup first polled Americans as to whether they approved of interracial couples. Only 4 percent did. In September 2022, fifty-five years later, Gallup found that 94 percent of Americans approved.[6]

Blacks today constitute 13 percent of the U.S. population. But far more than 13 percent of television ads feature blacks, often as interracial couples. Whites today clearly respond well to blacks serving as models for the purchase of products and services. Many movies also feature them in leading roles. These changes have occurred because America has undergone a moral transformation. Bigotry exists, but the nation as a whole is no longer racist.

Well then, why are whites wealthier than blacks?

Because of former racism and different cultural traditions. Whites initially came from England, where free-market capitalism, the best way for a nation to gain wealth, had long prevailed. The English also developed representative government, which helped to substitute compromise for force and violence.

American blacks originally came from Africa, where violence and slavery were common and free-market capitalism was not. As slaves in America, blacks had no opportunity to engage in free markets. Even after the Civil War, they had little opportunity to learn the cultural traditions

6. Erica Pandey, "The Rise of Interracial Marriage," Axios, September 7, 2022.

of whites because Jim Crow laws reduced them to poverty and prevented them from becoming professionals or entrepreneurs. After World War II, many American blacks gained wealth rapidly. But this came to a halt after 1970, when laws like the Great Society, the War on Poverty, and the War on Drugs were enacted. Unintentionally, those laws reduce the prosperity of America's poor, blacks included.

Government, universities, big corporations, and the media promote accusations of racism so that government may gain more control of peoples' lives: how we relate to each other, what we eat, what we drive, the temperatures of our homes and buildings, how much electricity we use, our industrial processes. I can understand why universities would want more of the nation's resources to be controlled by government, because the professors could advise government what to do. But why big corporations would want more of the nation's resources to be controlled by government escapes me. Do they not realize that totalitarian government officials would consider sources of power and wealth other than themselves to be a threat?

President Lyndon Johnson's so-called 'Great Society' began expanding greatly in the 1960s. Funny coincidence: The number of children born to unmarried mothers, both white and black, began expanding greatly in the 1960s. The main goal of the Great Society was the total elimination of poverty and racial injustice. Nice going, guys. The result has been quite the opposite. In fact, the long-term results of big-government policies are almost always opposite the intended results. Big government doesn't eliminate poverty; it causes poverty.

The most consequential racists in America are federal legislators since they assume that blacks can't make it without government's assistance. Of *course* blacks can make it without government assistance. But it would help if the government reversed numerous policies, like the Great Society, that make life worse and more expensive for the poor.

The folks at Black Lives Matter say that America discriminates against all minorities. Really? Whites are not the highest income group in America. Asians are. The average Asian family is upper income.[7] All too many whites, not to mention blacks, are waiting for government checks while the Asians are out working.

Shelby Steele, born in 1946, is a columnist and documentary film-maker. His grandfather was born a slave. He is a Senior Fellow at Stanford University's Hoover Institution, specializing in race relations, multiculturalism, and affirmative action. Steele wrote, "I grew up in segregated America, where it was hard to find an open door. It's harder now for young blacks to find a closed one." In 2018, he wrote, "A white-on-black shooting four years ago in Ferguson, Missouri, resulted in a lengthy media blitz. But thousands of black-on-black shootings in Chicago during those same four years gained little notice. Why? Because "the left gains power by fighting white evil, not black despair." Steele also wrote, "Bigotry exists, but it is far down on the list of problems that minorities now face."

The U.S. government wants Americans to believe that the nation is racist. This would enable the government to exercise ever more control over their lives. It's a bogus issue.

---

7. Stephen Moore, "No the United States is Not Systemically Racist," Washington Examiner, September 29, 2020.

CHAPTER 5

WHY THE MEDIA IS SO LIBERAL

MANY OF THE MOST PROMINENT American media are not in the news business; they're in politics. They omit bad news about Democrats and omit good news about Republicans. They want their viewers to vote for Democrats. Most Republicans are called 'far-right' Republicans. The great majority of democrats are Socialists, which is about as close to Communism and you can get. Are they called far-left Democrats, which they certainly are. Oh no, they're called just plain Democrats.

Why the bias? Because unless wrong-doing or sex is involved, free-market news is boring. Who cares what Mr. and Ms. Jones are doing to satisfy their daily needs? Who cares that Mr. Peters has been made CEO of Enterprise, Inc.? Also, it's difficult for media to keep track when important decisions are made by thousands of just plain citizens in a diverse, free-market, liberty-loving society. It's easier to keep track of the decisions made by top leaders in government. They affect almost everyone, and they can exert force. It's in the interest of the media to promote big government, even though that's not in the interest of the nation.

GOVERNMENT MOTIVATIONS

In the private sector of a free-market economy, profits are a key motivation. If an activity makes a profit, those who benefit want to produce more of it. If it doesn't profit, they try something else. Public-sector employees cannot evaluate themselves in those terms because government makes no profit. Government earns nothing. It simply incurs costs, dealing almost exclusively with other peoples' money.

Public-sector employees have four basic motivations. Here's the first:

Bureaucrats, who have the job for life and are rarely fired, don't try to truly *solve* social and economic problems. If a problem were solved, the bureaucrats involved would be left with nothing to do. Emotionally, that's almost as bad as not having a job. There are over eighty federal programs to help the poor. If any of them succeeded and poverty were wiped out, bingo, hundreds of thousands of bureaucrats would be idle for that purpose.

The second government motivation: Like everyone else, people in the public sector want higher pay. But higher pay means higher costs. In the private sector, higher costs mean less profit. The desire for profit creates a built-in regulator of costs, causing folks in the private sector to *minimize* costs. Bureaucrats make no profits. They have no such regulator. They're spending other peoples' money, and their costs are unrestrained.

The third motivation is what makes government unique: the use of force. People in the private sector are not permitted to force anyone to do anything. An employer can insist that the employee do something to continue getting paid. But the employee can refuse, quit the job, and find another. Government is different. Whoever fails to abide by its laws and regulations can be deprived of money, property, liberty, or even life. People who work for government enjoy having power over others. It's their thing. Over the decades, they have come to exercise altogether too much force.

The natural inclination of government officials and bureaucrats is to make government larger and more powerful, giving them more jobs, more pay, and more power. It's easier to accomplish these goals if they can persuade Americans that they're living in a crisis. COVID-19 provided an ideal opportunity. Government succeeded in scaring people in a manner that was wholly unjustified. As a result, American governments, especially the feds, are exercising more power now than they ever have, causing no end of harm. And they're salivating for yet more power.

Here's the final government motivation: With no profits, blame is especially prevalent among people who work for government. They try hard to avoid feeling they've been wrong. This is playing out now in a big way. Beginning in April 2020, the Federal Reserve expanded the money supply too rapidly. A year or two later, rapid inflation resulted. Economist Milton Friedman, now deceased, explained that interest rates have little to do with inflation. A general rise in prices, which we call inflation, has only one cause: the excessive creation of money. Reducing inflation has only one solution: cutting the money supply. To avoid feeling that they were at fault, employees of the Federal Reserve Bank have persuaded themselves and, with the media's help, tried to persuade everyone else that the rapid inflation was caused by supply-chain problems, the war in Ukraine, higher housing costs, or whatever else they could think of. They avoid acknowledging the actual cause: their own creation of too much money.

Because of the disastrous Covid lockdowns, the federal government passed out huge amounts of cash to American citizens. Most people, including those in the media, consider this to have been inflationary. It was not. The only thing that creates overall inflation is the excessive creation of money. If the Federal Reserve were truly independent of the legislature, as it purports to be, it would have refused to create excess money to support the Covid payments. The Fed would have taken a tremendous amount of political heat, of course. But if it had exercised such restraint, the legislature would have had to pay less Covid benefits, reduce other expenses, or add the Covid welfare payments to the national debt, probably complaining about it all the way. Without the excessive new money, inflation would not have occurred. It did not occur in Switzerland, China, and Japan. Those nations limited the creation of money all along.

Bigger government and more power are the overwhelming desire of most people in government. The Russian Communists in 1917 did not gain power to achieve a revolution. Quite the opposite: They achieved a revolution to gain power. Increasing the government's size and power is the top priority of American governments, especially the feds.

GOVERNMENT AGENCIES CAPTURED

Incapable of reform, big government must be pulled out by the roots. Some agency heads have had every intention of reforming the agency they were expected to run, but they were undermined by the bureaucrats. The bureaucrats, in turn, have been "captured" by big companies in the private industries they supposedly regulated, those companies having had established relationships with lifetime bureaucrats and the reporters who cover the industry. The companies have used the power of the bureaucracy to beat back competitors in their own industry.

Agency-capture has been going on for decades, regardless of who was president. The Department of Housing and Urban Development is captured by real estate interests; the Food and Drug Administration is captured by the pharmaceuticals and food retailers; the Department of Agriculture by agribusiness, the Department of Education by the teachers' unions. On it goes with the Pentagon, Federal Trade Commission, Department of Commerce, office of the U.S. Trade Representative, Department of Labor, Department of Energy, and most of the rest of the 200 plus agencies and bureaus in Washington.

Let's pull those agencies out by the roots and close them down.

Well, you say, if government no longer regulates anything, those same companies will capture the people in the private sector who endeavor to regulate them.

They'll certainly try. But the task will become much more difficult. Here's why:

- The regulators won't be centered in Washington, with a bureaucracy that can't be fired.
- Formal regulations often won't be necessary. With government out of the way, the people will become increasingly well-informed. Their voices and their buying decisions will often serve as regulators. Big government makes people apathetic – just the way the bureaucrats like it. When government is reduced, people get smart.
- With less government to champion, the media will join in the effort to combat the effort by big companies to impede small ones.

For centuries, stock and commodity exchanges in America and the United Kingdom administered complicated regulations that worked well without government involvement.

Government payments to some groups and not to others arouse resentment. People respond by trying to beat the government's system, which promotes selfishness. If government is greatly reduced, people would take responsibility, not only for their own actions, but also for the entire society. Less government means more selflessness.

Donald Trump is now being pursued vociferously to prevent him from being reelected president. Here's the main reason why: At the end of Trump's first term, he fully intended in his second term to make at least some of the federal bureaucracy fall under the control of the president and give the president the right to fire them.

In my opinion, Donald Trump was cheated out of victory in the 2020 election. I believe the primary cheating took place in the six or seven states in which the governorships, legislatures, police, and courts had been controlled for years by Democrats. They expected and were prepared for a Trump victory. But they were not prepared for a resounding Trump victory. Late on election night, someone (probably Barack Obama, in my opinion) instructed all those states to stop counting, giving time for measures to be taken to deal with the crisis, including truckloads of fake ballots. Later that night, ballot counting resumed, but the watchers were forcibly prevented from observing the count.

MAKE HEALTHCARE BETTER AND CHEAPER

U.S. healthcare is too costly because government is so deeply involved. Here's a key solution: Health insurance policies would have large yearly deductibles of several thousand dollars. Policyholders would pay *all* their healthcare costs for the year up to the amount of the deductible. The costs for the rest of the year would be paid by the insurance company, (not government or government insurance). By paying their own costs, policyholders would become familiar with the prices of healthcare products and services, just as they are with the other products and services they buy. If they were paying the costs themselves, people would think twice whether they needed professional healthcare, and if so, what kind. Competition between suppliers would drive the costs down, probably way down.

Competition between healthcare suppliers doesn't occur now because consumers don't directly pay the costs. Co-pays have no bearing on the choice of products. The government and/or the insurance companies pay the costs, and it's not in their interest to reduce them; they like that big-money flow. Few doctors know the true costs. In hospitals, just about the only people who know the costs are the clerks in the finance offices, and it's not in their interest to create controversy by refusing to pay suppliers whose costs are excessive.

Legislatures should sharply limit the penalties from medical malpractice lawsuits. This would reduce the insurance premiums of physicians and reduce the number of tests required by physicians, cutting costs. Restricting the penalties would also make it possible for clinics to write legally binding restrictions on liability. For minor health problems, clinics would charge less than physicians and far less than emergency rooms. With liability issues settled, low-cost clinics would become widespread.

The government's judgments about healthcare have been wrong all too often, especially regarding Covid. The Centers for Disease Control, Federal Drug Administration, and National Institute of Health, for example, arranged for dangerous treatments called vaccines. They faked safety trials to rush the vaccines into use and prevented people from using effective, inexpensive drugs. They shielded pharmaceuticals companies from lawsuits. In outrageous conflicts of interest, U.S. officials and senior bureaucrats took substantial payments from the pharmaceuticals companies for approving the vaccines. They failed to inform the public that the chances of people over seventy dying from Covid were small and that the chances of people under seventy dying from Covid were minute. (The infection survival rate for people over 70 is 95 percent. For people under 70, it's 99.95 percent.)[8] They failed to urge most people to get out and about, to gain immunity, the best and most lasting kind of protection. Covid transmits readily, but it is not deadly. To expand its size and power, the government created unjustified fear about Covid.

Under U.S. patent 7776521, the U.S. Centers for Disease Control and Prevention (CDC) owns the entire genetic content of the Covid virus. It also owns patents for detection methods and for a kit to measure viruses. In 2007, the CDC filed a petition with the patent office to keep its coronavirus patent confidential. The CDC thus controls who can make inquiries about it. Without authorization, one cannot look at the virus, cannot measure it, or make tests for it.

---

8. Dr. Jayanta Bhattacharya, "Facts – Not Fear – will Stop the Pandemic." AIER, December 6, 2020.

If SARS-CoV is natural, then the patent is illegal because naturally occurring DNA is not patentable. If the virus is manmade, the patent violates biological weapons treaties and laws. Either way, the CDC has probably engaged in illegal activity.

In 2013, the National Institutes of Health (NIH) suspended the funding of research on coronavirus, on the basis that such gain-of-function research was too risky to continue. This included funding to Harvard University, Emery University, and the University of North Carolina at Chapel Hill. The NIH made the funding pause voluntary, however, not mandatory. Then, in 2014, after many people had become concerned about the safety of gain-of-function research into coronaviruses, the NIH, under the leadership of Dr. Anthony Fauci, offshored that research to the Wuhan Institute of Virology in China. The funding from the NIH to China thereafter was not sent in a straightforward manner, however. It was instead funneled through front organizations such as the EcoHealth Alliance, so that the NIH could maintain that it had not funded the research.

Reports of Covid deaths have been greatly exaggerated. The federal government pays hospitals $34,000 for putting Covid patients on ventilators and $48,000 if the hospital patient dies from Covid. When deaths occur, it is in the financial interests of the medical community to declare, correctly or not, that the death was caused by Covid. Reported deaths from heart attacks, cancer, and other normal causes fell significantly during the Covid outbreak. It is highly likely that the number of such deaths did not actually fall, but rather that the causes of the deaths were misreported.

Along with social and news media, the government censored its critics. They frightened the public with absurd projections and forced them to take vaccines. They imposed lockdowns which destroyed livelihoods and small businesses and damaged the economy. The rules hindered children from development and learning, especially in public schools, and increased the incidents of suicide. New York, New Jersey, Massachusetts, and Michigan, which set up the most draconian of the state lockdowns, were the worst-performing in Covid deaths per capita. Wyoming, Utah, South Dakota, and North Dakota, which did not lock down, were among the best in Covid deaths per capita.[9]

Taiwan imposed fewer Covid controls than Sweden and far fewer than the United States. Taiwan has a population of close to 24 million and a high population density of 1,739 people per square mile. Guess how many Covid deaths the Taiwanese suffered: seven. And these were people over 40 with the majority having preexisting health conditions.[10]

Government fostered the widespread use of masks. Viruses, being microscopic, are not impeded by regular masks. Thousands of viruses could march arm in arm through each of the holes in a mask. No matter whether people breathe through the mask or from around the edges of the masks, the masks don't prevent the transmission of viruses. But viruses do adhere to the interior of a mask, building up in greater quantity than if no mask were used, adding to the danger. Masks also hide facial expressions, impeding social interaction, which is especially damaging for children.

During Covid, patients to some extent lost their rights when they entered hospitals, in effect becoming prisoners. Hospitals were given huge bonuses by the government if they used remdesivir and if they ventilated patients. Both of those treatments are dangerous.

Beginning when the vaccines were first brought to the market, the government told us we should not rely on natural immunity to protect against the virus and that we should get vaccinated. The officials received substantial benefits from the pharmaceuticals for promoting vaccines, a shocking conflict of interest.

The Society of Actuaries reported in August 2022 that people of

9. Ethan Yang, "A Closer Look at the States that Stayed Open," AIER, August 24, 2020.
10. Amelia Janaskie, "The Mystery of Taiwan" AIER, November 19, 2020.

working age had suffered a 20 percent uptick in excess deaths due to vaccine mandates. The immune systems of millions of people have been wrecked by multiple shots of messenger RNA (mRNA) drugs. Our immune systems are less able to suppress cancers. Spike proteins, which linger in human bodies for more than a year after vaccine shots, have damaged cardiovascular systems, caused neurological and brain damage, and been hurtful to pregnant women. Since the vaccine mandates, funeral directors have noticed a significant increase in the clotting of blood among the deceased. Since Covid vaccine injections began, there has been a worldwide increase in deaths and infertility. The vaccines were not invented by science in pursuit of good health. They were invented by big government in pursuit of bigger government.

Covid was a "gain-of-function" development in a Chinese laboratory. For the U.S. government to help finance this potential danger to mankind was outrageous.

Great Britain has benefited from a substantial increase in the number of people who have switched from combustible cigarettes to vaping. Introduced some twenty years ago, vaping is far less harmful than smoking tobacco, since it contains none of the cancer-causing tar that results from burning tobacco. There have been no reported deaths from nicotine vaping anywhere in the world. Thousands of vaping products are offered in the UK, with various choices of flavors and nicotine strengths. Fruit flavors are especially popular. In the U.S., the Federal Drug Administration (FDA) has authorized only a few vaping products, all of them tobacco flavored.[11] The primary purpose of the FDA during Covid was not to save lives, but to expand government's size and power.

Government should do nothing about viruses. It should, in fact, do nothing about health in general. Government is grossly unreliable, because its primary purpose is nearly always to make government big-

---

11. Martin Cullip, "United Kingdom Data Show the U.S. Public is Badly Served by the FDA." Inside Sources, September 12, 2022. (Taken from the Web.)

ger and more powerful. It purported to reduce Covid deaths. But its lockdowns caused many deaths, due to drug overdoses, depression, and suicide. The private sector would handle health matters far more effectively, with better care and much reduced costs.

GOVERNMENT DRUG TESTING COSTS LIVES

Government testers have kept some drugs off the market for years to avoid possible blame. More lives have been lost because of the delays than have been saved by the government ensuring that the drugs are safe. Some patients face death if they don't receive an experimental drug. "Nope," say the bureaucrats, "Can't have it. Might not be safe." They're talking about patients who are almost certain to die soon anyway. This attitude displays the common bureaucratic fear of being wrong, not to mention a grievous lack of common sense. If private companies did the testing, there'd be fewer deaths and lower costs, a nice combination.

In addition to safety, the government also tests whether a drug works better than its competition. Most other products are not tested by government for how well they work. Why drugs? Private companies should just check for safety and leave it to doctors and patients to decide what works, cutting significant costs.

DOCTORS SHOULD BE CERTIFIED
BY THE PRIVATE SECTOR

A person is not considered a doctor unless a state government says so. The public would be better served if government had nothing to do with it. One association might declare that a person is a Class A doctor, signifying that he or she has had a high level of training and could charge high fees. Another person might be a Class B doctor, who's had less training and could charge lower fees. There might be many grades of doctors.

Members of the public could decide what level of care they need and how much they're willing to pay. This would probably improve the overall quality of care as well. Today's monolithic organization of doctors, heavily influenced by the government, came out with opinions about Covid that were drastically wrong. Those opinions are still causing big health problems, some of them long term.

LAWYERS THE SAME

Lawyer organizations are quick to pounce on non-lawyers who want to charge modest fees for writing wills. No, they must go through unnecessary legal training, paid for with higher prices. The lawyers say they must maintain a high level of service. Yeah sure; what they really want are confiscatory fees. The public should be allowed to choose the level of lawyer training they need and how much they're willing to pay. If America's government sector were significantly cut back, as it should be, the need for lawyers would greatly diminish. Some of them might become mediators, helping people resolve conflicts outside of courtrooms, reducing the need for trials.

When people suffer because of someone else's mistake, damages should be paid, of course. But million-dollar damages for the equivalent of a stubbed toe are absurd. Damages should be capped. Juries are inclined to award excessive damages simply because, "They're paid by an insurance company, and those guys have plenty of money." But the money comes from somewhere. Some doctors pay sky-high premiums for their liability insurance policies because of exorbitant damages the insurance companies were required to pay. To cover that cost, the doctors raise their fees. When any part of the economy has unreasonable costs, those costs are ultimately paid by plain folks like you and me.

Tort lawyers take home about a third of tort damages. They live high off the hog and are among the largest contributors of campaign gifts to legislators, to retain the system that benefits them so excessively. An appropriate stand for tort damages should be reasonableness.

If government were cut back to 5 percent or less of the GDP and legislators were limited to single terms, lobbying to government would fall to near zero. Lobbying in the private sector would then increase. Lobbying in the private sector has a different name: It's called "advertising."

MORE ABOUT MONEY

Fabricating a paper dollar costs only a few pennies, but it's sold for a dollar. Better yet, fabricating a $100 paper dollar costs the same few pennies, but it's sold for $100. Best of all, creating a $10,000 bank deposit costs virtually nothing because it's electronic. Nice work if you can get it. This source of profit is called "signiorage." To protect it, the U.S. Treasury has established a monopoly. Only dollars can be used to settle debts, and only the government can earn the seigniorage.

Just a tiny portion of our money consists of paper and coins. Almost all of our money consists of numbers in bank accounts. Here's where those numbers come from: Assume that the Federal Reserve Bank bids higher than anyone else for Treasury securities, inducing me to sell my $10,000 of Treasury Bills. Through intermediaries, the Fed writes $10,000 in my bank account. That's new money. The only physical presence is the ink to write the number, and there's little of that because the process is electronic.

Let's say that you, dear reader, then obtain a loan of $6,000 from my bank, made possible by the increase in the bank's reserves from the Fed's previous $10,000 deposit. The percentages of new reserves that banks lend out may vary. The $6,000 created by my bank is also new money.

You deposit this in your bank, which then lends $4,000 to a third person, who deposits it in her bank. The banking system now has $20,000 of new money ($10K, plus $6K, plus $4K). On it goes, with each bank lending a portion of its new reserves. By the time the final dollar is lent, another $10K of new money will be created, making a total of $30,000. Under the current system, the money created by the banks depends on the Fed having initially created new reserves.

When the money supply increases faster than the supply of goods, the nation's general price level rises one to two years later. The Fed has created far too much money over the years. An item bought for $1.00 in 1913, when the Federal Reserve was created, would cost $30.39 today. Economies of all nations are healthier when the value of their currency remains level.

A newspaper headline, and many similar headlines, reads as follows: "Rising Housing Costs Drive Up Inflation." Sorry, rising housing costs do no such thing. If the money supply stayed the same, higher housing prices would cause the prices of *other* goods and services to *fall*. Picture a kid in a sandbox. If he pushes the sand to create a ridge, the area from where he pushed it is lower, since the amount of sand in the sandbox has remained the same. In the economy, assuming the money supply has not changed, a rise in prices of one sector causes the prices of other sectors to decline. A general rise in prices nationwide occurs only if the Federal Reserve Bank creates an excess of money.

In 2022, the Fed did not just lower the pace of money-supply growth. For the first time in decades, it turned the money-supply growth sharply *negative.* This will probably cause a recession in 2024. (This book is being finalized in January 2024.) The Fed has also raised interest rates, perhaps unaware that interest rates have little to do with inflation. Milton Friedman, as mentioned, explained that the excessive creation of money is the sole cause of inflation. The government has gone out of its way to maintain that Friedman is no longer running the show. He never did run the show, of course; he just offered solid judgments and opinions. But it's a shame he isn't running the show now.

The Federal Reserve's intrusions have created great harm by increasing the economy's volatility. The poor were hurt most because they were laid off in great numbers during the deep downturns. Other than atomic explosions, little destroys a nation faster than inflation.

Attempts to even out the economy, which the Fed endeavors to do, cannot help but make things worse. Let's say the 330 million Americans average two retail purchases a day. That's 660 million transactions. But most retail products have long supply lines. The new Boeing 737 Max, for example, has 600,000 parts, some of which themselves contain components. These items have supply chains of various lengths, but they all begin with land, a mine, a drill, a farm, a forest, a tropical jungle, a desert, an ocean, a river, a lake, or a lab. Each time an item passes from one owner to another, there's a transaction with a price, a transaction that benefits both sides. With free-market capitalism, each price reflects actual supply and demand conditions right there and then. The numerous transactions adjust the economy in a manner that is timelier and more appropriate than any information government can assemble to make its adjustments.

The most outrageous attempt to improve the economy was that of President Herbert Hoover. With the support of Congress, he raised tax rates and tariffs substantially and interfered with the economy with unprecedented government activism, supposedly to engineer a healthier economy.[12] Whoops, the result was the Great Depression.

The Federal Reserve Bank was created to reduce the economy's volatility that had been experienced in the nineteenth century. It was expected to cut the money supply to slow down the economy before the peaks and increase the money supply to speed it up before the troughs. It failed miserably. Instead of subduing the peaks and valleys, the Fed made them worse. The reason: No one knows when the economy is peaking and when it's bottoming. No one *can* know, at least not consistently. Oh

12. Steve Forbes, "Less Can Be More – Much More," Forbes, May 2020

sure, everyone knows after the fact, when they look at the charts. But no one can *predict* the changes. The 400 PhDs in economics who work for the Federal Reserve Bank, can't do it any better than everybody else.

The volatility in the nineteenth century may have been partly caused, directly or indirectly, by the federal government's huge subsidies to the railroad builders. There are time lags of various lengths between causes and economic effects. No person and no government agency, no matter how capable their computers, can keep up with the multiple causes, multiple effects, and variety of time lags, all operating together. It's a jumble out there, too complex for anyone to deal with except free markets. Free markets contain the intuition and wisdom of the millions of people who participate in them. This is far greater knowledge and intuition than those of any person or group of people who endeavor to meddle with the economy.

Even now, Congress should reduce its mission of the Federal Reserve Bank. Congress requires the Fed to maintain stable prices – Ha! It also requires the Fed to maintain maximum employment. When this second requirement was enacted, the legislators assumed that the Fed could do the job. They were wrong. It is beyond the capacity of anyone to interfere with the economy to maintain maximum employment. The Fed should be relieved of this requirement. Money should be created at a steady pace as the population grows.

Okay, who should create our money? Here are two alternatives:

The first alternative: The Treasury Department would continue its monopoly of the dollar, and the Federal Reserve Bank would be abolished. Only the dollar continues as the U.S. currency. The Treasury might create a certain amount of new dollars every day, in the same percentage as the average growth of the population. Congress would prevent the Treasury from interfering with the economy in any other way.

If government is significantly reduced, a major source of economic volatility would be removed. The dollar would be backed by gold, with the price of gold set free. The price would probably fluctuate by minuscule amounts from minute to minute. Even over the long term, it would fluctuate little, mostly because of how much new gold is being mined, how much is being diverted for manufacturing, clothing, works of art, and how much is being buried with people who have died. The Treasury would own enough gold to serve as backup for the dollar. But a large part of the federal government's huge cache of gold could be sold in return for the new owners taking over portions of the national debt.

"Gold backing" means that the owner of a gold-backed currency can choose at any time to exchange it for a specific physical amount of gold, measured in ounces per dollar. The gold would be owned by and provided by the currency's creator, in this case, the U.S. Treasury. Gold-backed dollars would retain a buying power that's close to level over time.

Congress would have the power to worsen this favorable mission of the Treasury. The only effective means of preventing such a change would be a knowledgeable desire by the people for a steady increase in the money supply and no other government involvement in the economy.

Here's the second alternative for supplying our currency: Again, the Federal Reserve Bank would be abolished. But this time the government's monopoly over the dollar would be removed. (The Constitution *authorizes* the federal government to provide a monetary system but does not require it. The government would refuse the honor.)

There would be many currencies created by banks, including perhaps BancAmericaDollars and MorganDollars. Each bank would design its own bills and coins, and each bank is likely to offer accounts in more than one currency. Each currency would be freely exchangeable with every other. The people could choose which currencies are most convenient and best hold their value.

Currencies backed by gold would be especially popular among creditors because the creditors want the buying power of the money they are repaid to be roughly the same as the buying power of the dollars they lent. (If you have a bank deposit, you're a creditor, because the bank owes you the money back.) Banks that provide gold-backed currencies would own gold in sufficient quantities to serve as the backup.

Privatizing the currency markets would delegate monetary policy to the people. Having several currencies would be inconvenient, but Europe lived with this for years. The competition between those who provide the currencies would prevent them from overdoing it. Some banks might seek to maximize their profits by producing too much of their money. But inflation of that currency would result. People would stop using it, bringing the bank's seigniorage to a halt. The competition is a non-government regulator, a restraint. Having no competition, the Federal Reserve Bank is unrestrained, which is why the dollar's buying power has deteriorated so.

I would like to favor the second alternative above, because, with few exceptions, the more important a function, the greater the need for government to stay clear of it. A monetary system that suppresses inflation is certainly a crucial function. Nevertheless, I do favor the first alternative, because it retains a single U.S. currency. The dollar is much used in international trade, especially for purchases of oil. This is of considerable benefit to the United States.

From 1837 to 1863, private banking, with numerous currencies, thrived in the United States. The economy also thrived, without inflation. Numerous individual and corporate evaluators succeeded in identifying which banks were safe and held their value. The public cared about the risks and was knowledgeable about them. The public loses such caring and such knowledge when government takes over. Oh, the government seems to have it all in hand. But then, suddenly, it doesn't, and conditions quickly become worse than if the government had never become involved in the first place.

How can the economy's volatility realistically be reduced: By cutting back America's three levels of government from 40 percent to 5 percent or less of the Gross Domestic Product (GDP). Without interference from any part of government, the economy would become far less volatile.

STOCK MARKET PERILS

If you dabble in the stock market after the government is reduced, don't get your hopes up about the reduction of risks. The economy would be less risky, but stocks would not because the price-earnings ratios of stocks would rise. PEs of 60 or higher might become the norm. Any limited volatility that remains in the economy would cause stock prices to swing up and down as much as ever. If you buy and sell, you'd still be a loser.

How could it be otherwise? If most investors were consistently right, people would borrow up to their eyebrows, throw the money into the market, and come out zillionaires in short order. The people of the world can't improve standards of living that quickly. The stock market isn't a living organism, of course, but here's a good way to understand the issue: The stock market must make most short-term investors wrong.

The majority of those who buy commodity futures do us all a favor by losing most of the time. They enable the producers of commodities usually to sell their products in the futures markets at profits. This reduces the risks of the producers, cutting the costs of supplying us with the basic materials from which the products we use are fashioned.

Many stock investors, together with people in the investment industry and the business media, believe they can process business news and predict what the stock prices will do. They cannot, at least not consistently. They can't do it any more than the Federal Reserve Bank can predict when the economy is peaking and bottoming.

One might expect investment experts who manage mutual funds to hold the most cash at market tops, to minimize losses during the subsequent bear market, and to hold the least cash at market bottoms, to benefit from the ensuing bull market. Sorry, they don't succeed at either time. As a group, mutual fund managers, like most investors, hold the least cash at market tops, when the economic news is good and everyone is bullish, and they hold the most cash at market bottoms, when the economic news is poor and everyone is bearish. Those embattled experts are just people after all.

Who are the investors who fail to profit consistently? Why, it's the people who buy and sell stocks or mutual funds or Exchange Traded Funds – the very people catered to by the investment industry and the business media.

Who are the minority, who profit consistently from stocks over the long term? Those who buy and *hold* a variety of stocks. They may sell when they need the money for other purposes, of course. But otherwise, they just hang in there, relying on the work performed by the people of the world to improve living standards at a modest pace over the long term.

Successful investors would probably not buy individual stocks. They would buy classes of stocks, such as mutual funds or ETFs. They would adjust their portfolios no more often than every year-and-a-day, to achieve long-term capital gains. They would sell the classes of stocks that have done well and buy more of those that have performed poorly to bring the proportions back to the original percentages. Mind you, these adjustments would not be governed by earnings expectations or economic news. The investors would be reacting only to the changes in values, selling a little of the groups that have done well and buying a little more of those that have not. When the news is bad and everyone is bearish, successful investors might turn off the news for a while making it easier to avoid joining the crowd and selling.

CHAPTER 6

HOW TO ADVANCE PEACE REALISTICALLY

GOVERNMENTS MAKE WARS. PEOPLE DON'T. Political leaders enjoy the increased powers that wars require. They also bask in the patriotism they helped engender. But unless their patriotism is aroused, people don't care for wars. They certainly don't like to pay for them. The Federal Reserve Bank usually expands the money supply significantly to cover the costs of wars. One-to-two years later, the general price level rises. Inflation is damaging to any economy, especially hurting people living on fixed income. But when the U.S. government is involved and patriotism is aroused, the nation's self-image is on the line. Winning becomes essential, and the cost of the war remains largely uncounted.

The Vietnam War incurred 58,000 U.S. military deaths and cost a horrific $1 trillion in today's money. It was intended to stop the spread of Asian Communism. Surprise, surprise, Vietnam remains Communist, but it is now a big trading buddy of the United States. The war was fought for naught. It hurt America and devastated the Vietnamese. The only beneficiaries were the governments and the suppliers of weapons.

After Castro took over Cuba in 1959, President Eisenhower erred in breaking off relations. Now, almost seventy years later, the Cubans remain poverty-stricken and Castro cohorts remain in power. Instead, Eisenhower should have facilitated and encouraged American and international trade. The Cuban people would probably have become prosperous, and Castro would have been gone decades ago.

How can peace be advanced without everyone becoming benevolent? Answer: Delegate foreign policy to the private sector.

Wait a minute. Doesn't the Constitution require the federal government to defend the nation?

Yes, that's exactly what it should do: defend America against military incursions from Mexico, Canada, the sea, the air, and from space. This is considerably less than the federal government is doing now – preventing nations from invading other nations and trying to bring democracy to the entire world. Acting as the world's moral arbiter is prohibitively expensive. It also causes the United States, not only to appear arrogant and pretentious, but to *be* arrogant and pretentious.

The exploration of space should primarily be undertaken by people in the private sector. They should permit the government to piggyback on their efforts for purposes of defense. The government would be wise to allow the private sector to take the lead because the private sector would do the job better and quicker than the government.

Let's say that the government would like to achieve a certain form of space exploration, but funds cannot be raised in the private sector to accomplish it. Provided the nation is properly defended, the government should back off. The private sector does not strive for perfection. It endeavors to meet only those needs for which funds can be raised to supply it. Society is most successful in the long term when it accepts modest imperfection.

The government should retain exclusive control of weapons of mass destruction, with the capability to deliver them from U.S. bases, including submarines, long-range bombers, and missiles.

The U.S. Navy should no longer patrol the world's oceans. Instead, ship owners should arm their ships, enabling them to defend themselves. Armed good guys would greatly outnumber armed bad guys. Before long, people traveling on passenger ships would become accustomed to their ships being armed. Younger passengers would enjoy the potential excitement.

The U.S. government should not protect the lives of Americans abroad. This may not be all that threatening to the Americans, since most nations that put Americans in jeopardy could lose important sources of income.

Private parties should be allowed to buy conventional weapons and store them in America. But except for military training, they could not be used in America. The cost of weapons would fall because there would no longer be just one buyer who is spending other people's money,

Terrorist organizations in Mexico are a problem for America. Either the federal government or armed private Americans could deal with them – perhaps both. It's likely that military power provided by armed private Americans would be more effective than that of the federal government, simply because, as stated frequently in this book, government is the worst and most expensive way to accomplish almost anything.

The United Nations offers little more than gab sessions for dictatorships. America should leave the United Nations and require the UN to leave America.

Associations in the private sector might exchange representatives with other nations. But the U.S. government would no longer own embassies or exchange ambassadors.

A high-altitude atomic explosion would knock out the U.S. grid plus the nation's computers and electronic devices – a devastating blow which the government should certainly defend against. Most foreigners, however, would be reluctant to launch such a strike for fear of losing the U.S. as a major trading partner. If the American government stopped its interferences throughout the world, foreign interests would likely reduce their military capabilities.

Private parties could gather whatever information they wish. Trade, travel, and tourism would be their primary interests. If private Americans uncover a potential threat to America, it would be in their interest to warn the government.

When a foreign entity has a troubling issue with America, it would contact an appropriate American association. When private Americans have a troubling issue with a foreign party, they would contact whoever would seem most likely to solve the problem.

Private Americans might consider a controversial matter with another nation so important that they'd contemplate fighting for it. But if the opponents are an aroused citizenry which doesn't care about the costs, the Americans might recognize that they would lose and thus avoid fighting. Whatever they decide, they would not be protecting America's homeland. The nation's self-image would not be on the line. Conflicts would be small with the costs counted.

Private Americans could join Ukraine's fight against Russia or participate in military struggles anywhere in the world, perhaps as mercenaries, but only at their own risk and expense.

Russia's conquering of Ukraine would be a tragedy. But this does not mean that Russia would then take over all of Eastern Europe. Perhaps, tragically, one or two of those nations, but not all of them. Western Europe and the Americas are out of the question. Taking over people who do not wish to be taken over eventually causes political indigestion, especially when Russia might be resisted by private Americans who are armed. The free nations of the world would also build up their own military defense instead of relying on a bankrupt America to do it for them.

A Chinese takeover of Taiwan would not mean that Singapore and the Philippines would come next. Years ago, if America had backed off its military, private Americans had been armed, and the Philippines had built up its defense, China would probably not have gotten away with arming islands in the South China Sea. The world would likely be safer if military power were disseminated more equally throughout the free

44

world, instead of everyone relying on the U.S. America's nuclear power stand ready as a backup.

How many mistakes can Xi Jinping make before he turns China into a paper tiger? He has permitted a vast expansion of real estate debt. Real estate developers, including the biggest, Evergrande, have filed for bankruptcy, leaving apartments unbuilt that millions of people have paid for. With an irrational fear of Covid, Mr. Xi has locked down major cities, affecting millions of people. He has consolidated more and more of the economy into state hands, which ruins the economy of any nation that tries it. As is true with any nation, the bigger the government, the greater the gap between rich and poor. The gap in China is very wide indeed. China no longer raises enough food to feed its population. If it starts a war, its importation of food would likely be cut off. Since China for many years required families to have only one child, the nation no longer has a surplus of young men to fight a war lasting more than a few months. Eventually, the police, who are expected to enforce the laws, will identify more with the members of their families who are suffering and less with the people who are paying them. The big guy will then be out on his ear.

If the world's electronic industry had felt assured that the United States government would not defend Taiwan, it would not have placed such a large portion of the world's semiconductor manufacturing in that nation.

Let's say that China attacks Taiwan, and a U.S. aircraft carrier provides effective military resistance. China fires scores of missiles to take out the carrier. A few get through, killing the 6,000 members of the crew and aircrew. You don't think American voters would accept this, do you? On the contrary, they would cry out, *"What the hell were you doing? Taiwan is not that important to us!"*

U.S. admirals may believe that America's extraordinary carrier groups can bluff opponents and not lose a carrier. If private Americans fight abroad, such muddle-headed thinking would be reduced because their own lives and money would be on the line.

Delegating foreign policy to private Americans would probably reduce conflict throughout the world. It would certainly reduce the cost of the American military.

CHAPTER 7

IT'S THE *RATES* OF TAX THAT COUNT

WHEN THE GOVERNMENT RAISES TAX *rates*, the press refers to it as "raising *taxes*." This is misleading. Government does not control its tax revenues; it controls only the *rates*. The revenues depend on how the taxpayers react to the tax. If the rate is raised and they don't mind it, fine, the revenues increase. But if the taxpayers do mind the rate increase, they might reduce their hours of work and cheat modestly so that the government's revenues stay even. If the taxpayers really mind the rate increase, they might reduce their work and cheat a great deal, causing the government's revenues to fall below what the government was taking in before the rate hike was passed.

Raising the tax rates and making government bigger causes more of the nation's wealth to flow through the government. This reduces wealth and hurts the poor more than the rich. In part, the poor are hurt because the rich have less money available to create jobs.

By the same token, lowering tax rates and making government smaller helps the poor more than the rich.

After World War I, the allies, especially France, imposed reparations on Germany that were high but not ruinous. The German government made a crucial mistake. To pay the reparations, they kept the income tax rates high. Most taxpayers are willing to suffer high tax rates during war-time, but not in peacetime. When Germany sustained the high tax rates after the war, government revenues did not remain the same; they went down, and the economy suffered grievously. To pay the reparations, the German government made another mistake; they felt they had no choice but to inflate the currency. The printing presses producing cash went into overtime. The people had to push wheelbarrows full of cash just to buy a few groceries. The mark became worthless, and this made peoples' savings worthless. A few years later, unfortunately, substantial increases in U.S. tariffs by President Hoover and the U.S. Congress significantly reduced international trade. In all, the loss of WWI, the disappearance of retirement savings, and the reduction of international trade caused the dispirited German people to choose a psychopath as their leader. Tragically, this led to the killing of over 20 million people and another losing war.

Another government requirement resulted in profound difficulties that have lasted for two thousand years. During the Medieval Period, the Roman Catholic Church was accepted as government in matters of morality. In AD 314, the Church forbade clerics from charging interest on loans. In 1179, it applied the same requirement to laymen. This suppressed economic activity. It also made it difficult for monarchs to fight wars, which they felt called upon to do frequently. Whom could they borrow from to pay for the wars? Ah-*ha*, the Jewish religion did not prevent Jews from charging interest. The Jews thus became heavy lenders and grew wealthy doing so. But they also earned the enmity of the gentiles, especially the monarchs, who were unable or unwilling to repay the loans. In 1290, Edward I expelled all Jews from England. In 1492, the same year Columbus discovered America, Ferdinand and Isabella expelled the Jews from Spain. Unfortunately, the enmity against Jews has persisted to the twenty-first century.

HOW TO CUT FUNDING FOR THE POLICE

Reducing the funding of police is a fine idea, but only under the following conditions:

- Allow people to carry semi-automatic weapons, hidden or not, without licenses. Armed good guys would outnumber armed bad guys, enabling the public to some degree to police itself. Weapons training would be widespread. The police and the courts, counseled by mental health professions, would have the right to prevent some of the mentally ill from carrying weapons and possibly force them to remain in mental institutions. The mental institutions would be owned within the private sector, but since the operators would be exercising force, they would have to be backed by the courts.

- Terminate the disastrous war against drugs. Schools would teach about the problems with drugs.

- Legalize prostitution. The criminalization of any industry raises the prices and attracts people who charge high prices because they're willing to disobey the law. If the criminalization is lifted, some of the bad guys might become reasonably good guys.

- The political pressure to create police departments came from businesses that wanted to avoid paying premiums for casualty insurance. The businesses lobbied to create police departments, forcing the cost onto the public. To cut down on current police costs, businesses that don't have proper insurance against physical loss, theft, and liability should be prevented from obtaining financing. A consortium of insurance companies, banks, and finance companies would agree on the proper conditions.

- Cameras at intersections would be operated by a consortium of insurance companies. If a driver has disobeyed the stop sign, the car owner would receive a ticket in the mail plus a notice from the insurance company that his or her insurance premiums have been raised.

A COUP IS IN THE WORKS

Haven't you heard? America is undergoing a coup. The Constitution requires that federal expenditures be proposed by the U.S. House and approved by the Senate. But up-to-date politicians don't bother with those silly requirements. Without Congressional approval, King Joseph I wants to spend upwards of $500 billion to cancel the student debt of some 40 million people. Never in American peacetime history has there been an executive action approaching this magnitude. Mr. Biden's intention has nothing to do with buying votes, of course. He wouldn't even *think* of that. [13]

---

13. WSJ, "A Half-Trillion-Dollar Executive Coup", August 25, 2022.

CHAPTER 8

HOW U.S. GOVERNMENTS HURT THE POOR

UNINTENTIONALLY, THE GOVERNMENTS OF THE United States cause long-term harm, especially for the poor. Here are examples:

The average return from each $1 spent on *lottery* tickets is 52 cents. Lottery players finance their tickets largely by cutting spending on necessities. In effect, lotteries work like a regressive tax. The poorest third of Americans buy more than half of all lottery tickets.[14] Numerous ads, mostly in poor areas, imply that a person can generate retirement income from lotteries. Sorry, the chance of achieving riches from a lottery is about the same as getting hit by lightning. When they lose, people can say, "Well, at least the money goes for education." Legislators are happy to vote lottery money for education without having to raise taxes for that purpose. They would be blamed for a tax. They are not blamed for the lotteries. But they certainly should be. Lotteries create poverty big time.

Nearly a quarter of Americans require *occupational licenses* to do their jobs. People already in the business lobby the state or local governments to require occupational licenses. Their purpose is to create a shortage of workers, thereby enabling high wages. Legislators aren't expected to create a shortage of workers intentionally, but in return for campaign gifts, they force themselves to comply. Laws create the short-

---

14. Arthur C. Brooks, "Powerbull: The Lottery Loves Poverty," WSJ, August 28, 2017.

ages by imposing fees and long periods of training to qualify for jobs. Few people on low income can afford those requirements. The high wages of workers cause the prices of their products or services to be high as well. People of low income are therefore hit twice: They can't qualify for the jobs, but they pay high prices when they buy the products. Occupational licenses benefit the prosperous and hurt the poor.

Rent control forces landlords to keep rent payments level for as long as the tenant remains in the apartment, despite the landlord's rising costs. The beneficiaries tend to be older, relatively prosperous tenants whose lives are stable. When they vacate, the landlord can raise the rent to market levels. Those high rents are paid by younger, less prosperous people who move frequently. Rent control helps the prosperous and hurts the poor.

Only about 2 percent of American workers are paid *minimum wage.* These include the wives of working husbands and kids still living with their parents. They are generally members of families whose total income exceeds $50,000 a year. Minimum-wage laws thus favor the prosperous and hurt the poor. Many small businesses are exempt from the federal minimum-wage laws. During the last forty years, every time the minimum wage was increased, hundreds of thousands of people were forced into jobs paying below the minimum. The higher minimums didn't increase unemployment. They simply forced people to obtain jobs that paid less than they received before, with fewer opportunities for advancement.[15]

Since residential land is expensive, most businesses avoid putting industrial facilities in residential areas. But after the door was opened to *government zoning,* there's been no end to it. Government zoning is unnecessary. Many aspects of housing are now highly regulated. This has raised costs and created significant housing shortages for people who are not rich, especially in California.[16]

15. Alan Reynolds, "When the Minimum Wage Rises, A Million More Fall Below Minimum," AIER, August 26, 2020
16. Jose Nino, Zoning: "The Nemesis of Housing Affordability," AIER, November 7, 2017.

The cost of *housing* and the cost of rents have soared in recent years, more so than the costs of most other products. Why? Because the production of housing is one of the most regulated and micro-managed industries in the industrialized world. With zoning and land-use laws, government planners control what sort of housing can be built and where. They tell us whether housing can be single-family or multi-family and whether we can rent out a bedroom to a non-relative. Urban renewal schemes bulldoze low-cost housing to make room for trendy shopping districts or government-owned housing. Often the pressure for such regulations comes from upper-income homeowners who don't want to live near a row of townhouses or apartment buildings and don't want more cars parked on the street. All this discriminates against the poor.[17]

Government regulations can make *childcare* unobtainable for people who need it most – those with low income. In Massachusetts, for example, childcare costs average about 65 percent of the average single parent's income. In Mississippi, the costs are less than 25 percent of single-parent income. Why the disparity? The regulations in Massachusetts are far more onerous than those in Mississippi. For example, Massachusetts mandates that childcare centers must have one staff member on hand for every three infants. In Mississippi, a staff member can care for five. People of lower income, who are most in need of jobs, are priced out of the childcare market, unable to earn outside income.[18]

The more a service is regulated, the higher the price, and the more it's generally available only to the prosperous. The people, not government regulators, should decide what quality of care they need in relation to how much they can pay.

Seacoast dwellers can buy *flood insurance* from the government with premiums that are unrealistically low. When floods occur, the gov-

---

17. Ryan McMaken, "Why Housing Cost Are So High," Foundation for Economic Education, December 24, 2020.
18. Max Gulker, "Why Does Child Care in Massachusetts Cost Four Times What It Does in Mississippi?" AIER, February 28, 2019.

ernment pays for the rebuilding. Legislators love this kind of law. The benefits are substantial and obvious. The costs on a per-capita basis are small and hidden, since they're paid from general tax revenues or added to the national debt. Seacoast dwellers are generally prosperous. Many of those who pay the costs are not. That's the way it goes with big government.

For half a century, the federal government has paid mostly rich farmers for growing *commodities*, especially corn. This has reduced the retail cost of those foods and thus contributed greatly to widespread obesity. Obesity has weakened many individuals, especially those who are less prosperous, and it has weakened the nation.

Social Security benefits terminate when the individual dies. Black men die at younger ages than white women. This means that Social Security taxes paid by black men support the longer lives of white women, but not the other way around.

Fentanyl is causing Americans no end of harm. More and better police work is needed, right? Wait a minute: That's what America has been doing with drugs for over half a century. The efforts have cost billions of dollars but failed anyway. The poor are hurt most since the drug war is fought primarily among the poor. Entrepreneurs who provide illegal drugs charge high prices because they're willing to disobey the law. They also increase the supply. With addictive products, bigger supplies induce bigger demand. If drugs were decriminalized, the entrepreneurs, no longer disobeying the law, could not charge high prices. Both the supply and the demand would fall. Money would be needed to teach Americans in schools about the dangers of drugs. But the end of the war against drugs would enable substantial savings in police work, and the benefits would be permanent, with the poor helped most.

Attempts to improve the economy by the *Federal Reserve Bank* have failed over and over. As discussed above, the Fed has created substantial economic swings that were especially detrimental to the poor, since so many of them had to be laid off during the downturns. The information the economy supplies itself by the millions of prices arrived at every day throughout the economy is timelier and more reliable than any information the Federal Reserve can assemble to plan its interferences.

For several decades, the Federal Reserve kept *interest rates unnaturally low.* Banks lent readily to the rich because they felt assured of repayment. They were less inclined to lend to the poor because the low interest rates didn't match the higher risks. The low rates therefore widened the gap between rich and poor.

Government welfare has transformed into massive entitlement that breeds dependence on government. Its inflexibility and lack of counseling, among other things, has caused too many black children to grow up in homes with no live-in father. Boys who grow up without fathers are more likely to fail in school and display violent behavior. Private sector welfare would have the flexibility to deal with the issue far better.

Faulty government policies caused the *2008 Credit Crisis* and the subsequent Great Recession. Among other policies, the government forced banks to lend at least 52 percent of their available mortgage money to people of low income. The government was deadly serious about it. To avoid being put out of business, the banks had to disregard incomplete and potentially fraudulent loan applications. Many of those mortgages defaulted, forcing banks to hold real estate they couldn't sell. The banks were also forced to "mark to market" their mortgage holdings. This meant the mortgages had to be valued in the bank's books according to what the mortgages could be sold "in current market conditions." But during the crisis, few existing mortgages were offered for purchase or sale, making current market conditions almost non-existent. To be sure of compliance, banks had to value their mortgages at ridiculously low prices, to the point where the bank assets became too small in relation to the bank's liabilities. Banks were forced out of the frying pan (required to accept fraudulent mortgage applications) and into the fire (unable to comply with net capital requirements). The Mark to Market rule was repealed, but not before numerous banks, especially in rural areas, were taken over by larger urban banks. Intentionally or not, big government usually benefits big companies more than small ones. It also causes serious economic downturns like the 2008 Credit Crisis and subsequent Great Recession, during which millions of people lost their jobs.

The *lockdowns* widened the gap between rich and poor. For example, the lockdowns closed great numbers of bars and restaurants. The millions of people who worked for those businesses were far from rich.[19]

New cars are costly. Used cars are not. As cars pass down the income ladder, sales by the rich and purchases by the poor transfer billions of dollars of automotive values from rich to poor. No one set up these transfers. They occur naturally because government is little involved in automobile marketing. Far larger transfers of values would occur with *real estate*, helping the poor enormously. But such free-market transfers of real estate do not occur because construction laws, environmental laws, zoning laws, banking, farming, water, and who knows what other laws are heavily involved with real estate sales.

In many U.S. cities today, the police can no longer guarantee *public safety.* Citizens everywhere should therefore be allowed to carry weapons without licenses. Even in poor areas, armed good guys would outnumber armed bad guys, reducing violence and social unrest. Weapons training should be widespread.

Blue states, like New York, Connecticut, and the District of Columbia, which have large and intrusive governments, have considerable inequality of income. Red states, like Wyoming, Utah, and New Hampshire, which have small and relatively unintrusive governments, have better equality of income. Hmm, it seems like the actual, long-term results of government policies are opposite to the intended results.

19. Stephen Moore, *"Lockdowns are the Great Unequalizer,"* Washington Examiner, December 22-29, 2020.

Decades of big government have caused the fabric of American life to deteriorate and widened the gap between rich and poor. Unintentionally, policies of American governments have especially hurt the poor. With the government sector greatly reduced, people should meet ever more of their needs successfully in the private sector.

GOVERNMENT HURTS EVERYONE EXCEPT GOVERNMENT WORKERS

According to the Labor Department, *women* across the workforce earn about 82.3 cents for every dollar earned by men. Women, in case you haven't noticed, are different from men. They bear children, bless them. But the time spent birthing and nurturing takes them away from their jobs, which disrupts the flow of work and increases the employer's costs. When mothers return to the job, they must be brought up to speed with new developments, also incurring costs for the company. Men gravitate to high-paying jobs that require strength. They're also drawn to danger-ous jobs, not only because they pay well, but because, well, men are different from women. Given these many factors, it seems fair that women should receive lower pay, even if they're doing the same job as men. But since human beings are an endangered species (see Page 71 below), women need all the help they can get.

Social Security has no investment reserves. Every dollar that comes in from the Social Security FICA tax goes out immediately for whatever purposes the government is spending that day. In one door and out the other. The Social Security Administration claims to have investment reserves, but these are not stocks, bonds, and other investments such as insurance companies hold. No, Social Security's investment reserves are simply federal bonds. It seems unlikely that those IOUs will be paid. Future Americans, who did not incur *our* debts, will balk at paying our Social Security bonds and will probably vote out of office legislators who insist on raising taxes to do so.

Social Security is not insurance. It's an income-transfer program, in which workers help to support retirees. But with the number of retirees growing faster than the number of workers, the system cannot help but fail. When that day comes, people who have paid FICA taxes all their lives may not receive the support they were expecting in retirement. It's a massive Ponzi scheme. Americans who depend most on Social Security benefits are the poor. Legislators may be aware of all this. But the cost of repairing the matter is so horrendous that they prefer the matter be considered after they retire. We'd be better off if government had nothing to do with retirement income.

The Jones Act, enacted over a hundred years ago, requires that goods shipped between U.S. ports and territories must be carried on ships built in America. They must be 75 percent owned and crewed by Americans, with the shipped goods never sold to foreign citizens. The act was supposed to protect U.S. shipping to and from U.S. ports. Ha! It has instead decimated U.S. shipping![20] The International Seaman's Union bestows ample campaign gifts to retain the devastating law. This seems shortsighted: If the Jones Act were repealed, the number of ships of all types operating in U.S. waters would increase greatly. Wouldn't some of those ships be crewed by members of the union? Maybe not. What do I know?

Government *guarantees of bank deposits* have caused depositors to care about the rate of interest and convenience, but not the money's safety. This explains, in part, why people have been impervious to the nation's unprecedented expansion of debt. If bank deposits were not guaranteed, wealthy depositors would take great interest in where banks are investing their money.

On federally funded jobs, contractors must pay construction workers *'local prevailing wages.'* This increases the wages of well-paid construction workers and requires an army of well-paid bureaucrats to enforce

20. WSJ, "'America First'? Kill the Jones Act," November 4, 2019.

the requirements. Who pays the costs? People who use the completed facility pay tolls that are higher than they would be without the arduous requirements. The numerous enforcers are paid by taxpayers.

If the government were much smaller and had nothing to do with labor costs, wages would be higher, not lower. This is because the economy would not be drained by a huge government that consumes wealth, creates no wealth, and impedes the private-sector's creation of wealth.

Tariffs and impediments to trade make citizens poorer. When the United States first became a nation, there was an immediate surge of economic activity because the U.S. Constitution removed all tariffs that had been imposed by the states on products imported from other states. If the U.S. currently repealed its tariffs and impediments to trade on products imported from other nations, it would benefit greatly, even if the opposing nations did not reciprocate. For many years, Hong Kong had the world's fastest-growing economy, partly because it had repealed all its tariffs. Most of the nations it traded with did not repeal their tariffs, but Hong Kong flourished anyway, more so than the others.

President Trump's most important policy mistake was to raise tariffs to achieve a positive balance of trade. This worked no better than mercantilism did in days of old. Positive trade balances do not cause a good economy. Besides, international trades are initiated by contracts, which are not agreed to unless both sides benefit. After Mr. Trump raised tariffs on steel, other nations reciprocated with their tariffs. As a result, the jobs lost among American companies that use steel greatly outnumbered the jobs gained among American companies that make steel.[21] Government should consider the balance of trade as none of its business.

Not just contracts, all financial transactions in the private sector are voluntary. If both sides do not benefit, the transaction does not occur. In contrast, transactions in the public sector are compulsory. America has too few of the former and far too many of the latter.

---

21. Phil Gramm and Pat Toomey, "Trump's Protectionist Failure," WSJ, March 3, 2021.

The *forfeiture of privately-owned assets* to benefit police departments is outrageous and should be terminated. [22]

The government collects a myriad of *statistics* that reveal social and economic problems which the government then endeavors to solve. Most government solutions have made things worse. The nation would be better off if all statistics were collected and paid for by the private sector.

The federal government has laid down a multitude of requirements regarding Covid. The requirements were not only wrong, they caused considerable physical and emotional harm.

Child Labor Laws have been way over-enforced, preventing teens from working a wide range of jobs, thereby limiting their knowledge and experience.

High tax rates cause more of the nation's income to flow to the government, whose laws and regulations reduce the creation of wealth. Government consumes wealth and inhibits its creation. Low tax rates cause more of the nation's income to flow to the private sector, increasing the creation of wealth.

Big government and high tax rates cause the rich to gain wealth faster than the poor. Small government and low tax rates enable the poor to gain wealth faster than the rich.

In the 1980s, Ronald Reagan reduced personal income tax rates substantially, boosting the economy and especially benefiting the poor.

In 2017, Donald Trump reduced corporate income tax rates substantially, boosting the economy and especially benefiting the poor. U.S. corporate tax rates had been the highest in the world. Numerous American corporations had moved their headquarters to other nations to avoid the ominous burden. But after the corporate tax rates were reduced, the corporations came home, and government revenues soared. Household incomes during the two years that followed rose by more than they

---

22. Stephen C. Miller, "Civil Asset Forfeiture Undermines Free Enterprise and Human Dignity," AIER, January 27, 2018.

had during the previous eight years. Wages for the bottom 10 percent of earners grew at double the rate that had prevailed during President Obama's second term. For the first time since 1972, the unemployment rate of blacks fell below 6 percent. The reduction of corporate tax rates was by far President Trump's most beneficial policy.

In 2007, the Index of Economic Freedom by the Heritage Foundation ranked the United States third, behind Hong Kong, Singapore, and Australia. In 2023, economic freedom in the USA had deteriorated, ranking the nation twenty-fifth. The twenty-four nations considered freer include Canada, Chili, the Czech Republic, Denmark, Estonia, Finland, Germany, Ireland, Latvia, Norway, South Korea, and Sweden. America's founders are rolling in their graves.

As economic freedom has diminished, U.S. governments have enacted laws and regulations, which, including all their ramifications, probably comprise millions of requirements, all backed by force. As government has exercised ever more force, the wealth of the rich and of the poor have become ever more unequal. The use of force by citizens in the streets, for robberies and other crimes, has also become far more common.

Regulations by the U.S. government constitute a hidden tax estimated to be $1.9 trillion each year. The economic annual burden of regulations on each U.S. household is estimated to be $14,615. This amounts to 20 percent of the average pre-tax household budget. Except for housing, it exceeds every item in that budget. The cost is estimated to exceed 40 percent of total federal spending.[23]

With few exceptions, government is the worst and most expensive way to accomplish almost anything. It is time for America's government sector to be greatly reduced and for individual liberty to hold sway.

Assume that services performed by government are privatized. But also assume that for a particular service, few people have expressed a need for it, and money can't be raised to supply it. That privatization

23. Competitive Enterprise Institute, Ten Thousand Commandments 2019

would not occur. Liberals would complain, "There's a need there, and you're not meeting it!"

True. But liberals endeavor to meet *every* need, which accommodates their primary goal: to make government bigger. Growing government often means adding costs to the national debt. The private sector does not strive for perfection. It endeavors to meet only those needs for which funds can be raised. Society is most successful in the long term when it accepts modest imperfection.

Here's the most common way that money is raised: Some smart cookie sees a need that others have not filled, raises funds, and arranges things to fill the need. He or she sees a profit potential and raises funds to make it happen. Many undertakings by entrepreneurs fail, ending up with losses, which the entrepreneur may be required to absorb. He or she takes a risk in making the effort.

Profits are the most important ingredient of a successful society. Without profits, a society is bound to fail. Profits enable the poor to join the middle class, or even get rich. Profit is not stealing, as liberals like to describe it. No, they want the *government* to grow, not the private sector. They want funds to be raised primarily by taxation.

Government makes no profits. It just incurs costs – lots and lots of costs.

The Bill of Rights was probably unnecessary. The U.S. Constitution provides that if the Constitution does not specifically authorize a particular power, the federal government must not do it. As mentioned earlier, government people have latched onto the general welfare clause and assumed on this basis that they are authorized to do anything they feel like doing. Our behemoth government hangs on those two words, general welfare. How about a Constitutional Amendment to expunge them? The private sector takes care of the general welfare far better than government can. People believe that America is going wrong. This isn't the private sector; it's the public sector which is too big and too intrusive.

The legislatures of the federal and state governments are housed in grandiose buildings that convey the impression that the laws enacted therein should be accepted as right and proper. Most of what government does, as demonstrated throughout this book, is wrong and improper. It seems fitting, therefore, that legislators should assemble for their deliberations in Quonset huts.

You may have spent some of your hard-earned money on gifts to charity to help the poor. Nothing wrong with that, of course. But there's another way of helping the poor. As this book makes plain, big government unintentionally causes poverty. Making government smaller and less intrusive would lift a huge burden off the shoulders of the poor.

How can one person make government smaller? Well, now that you ask, you might help by going to ArchieRichards.com and making a donation to help publicize this book, so that it may affect public policy for the better. I'll be right there with you. I don't spend much. I don't plan to spend much. Most of my royalties from the book for a long time will be plowed right back into publicity.

But there's a hooker: The government doesn't consider the book to be a charity. Contributions to publicize it are not deductible. You must make the contributions with after-tax income. But all is not lost. Government is America's primary creator of poverty. One dollar spent enabling the book to influence public policy for the better probably relieves as much poverty as many dollars given to tax-deductible charities.

America is hurting. America's poor are hurting. Well, they may be living passively on government doles. But it's outrageous that the government has converted millions of people into passive takers. Let's you and I and a whole lot of other people, by promoting this book, do what we possibly can to shrink the power of government. It's-too-big!

Chapter 9

Preventing School Massacres

A DERANGED PERSON GOES INTO a school and shoots as many people as possible. Is there no solution for this? Of course there is. Every adult employee of every school should carry a weapon and be trained in its use. As soon as a perpetrator displays a weapon, he or she would immediately be shot. As soon as most schools adopt such measures, most school massacres would come to a screeching halt. The same goes for massacres outside of schools. If everyone is armed, and weapons training is widely available, armed good guys would greatly outnumber armed bad guys.

GET GOVERNMENT OUT OF EDUCATION

The federal government pays schools for moving students up to the next grade, regardless of whether the students have learned what was expected of them in the previous grade. When a student is required to repeat a grade, the school receives no federal subsidy. As a result, too many students are moved up to the next grade regardless of poor results. Too many graduate from high school barely able to read. It's a built-in system set up by the government that gives rise to the government's expansion but insures the deterioration of education.

The cost of public education has soared. Since 1970, government spending on education increased by 368 percent, and that's *after* adjusting for inflation. The main reason: a tremendous increase in the number of education administrators and other education bureaucrats, most of them well paid. Have the results improved accordingly? Not on your life. The quality of education has deteriorated from kindergarten to graduate school. The scores are worst among the poor, making schools highly regressive. Over the past four years, reading and math proficiency collapsed, partly because the teachers unions insisted that public schools stay closed throughout Covid.[24]

See if you can pass the following final exam. This was reported by the *New Republic* on November 28, 2010:

EXAM GIVEN TO EIGHTH GRADERS IN SALINA, KANSAS, IN 1895

Grammar (Time, 1 hour)

1. Give nine rules for the use of capital letters.

2. Name the parts of speech and define those that have no modifications.

3. Define verse, stanza and paragraph.

4. What are the principal parts of a verb? Give principal parts of do, lie, lay and run.

5. Define case, illustrate each case.

6. What is Punctuation? Give rules for principal marks of Punctuation.

7-10. Write a composition of about 150 words and show therein that you understand the practical use of the rules of grammar.

Arithmetic (Time, 1.25 hours)

1. Name and define the fundamental rules of arithmetic.

---

24. Daniel J. Mitchell "Government Schools: More Bureaucracy, Lower Performance, and Higher Costs." AIER, February 15, 2021.

2. A wagon box is 2 ft. deep, 10 feet long, and 3 ft. wide. How many bushels of wheat will it hold?

3. If a load of wheat weighs 3942 lbs., what is it worth at 50 cts. per bu, deducting 1050 lbs. for tare?

4. District No. 33 has a valuation of $35,000. What is the necessary levy to carry on a school seven months at $50 per month, and have $104 for incidentals?

5. Find the cost of 6720 lbs. coal at $6.00 per ton.

6. Find the interest of $512.60 for 8 months and 18 days at 7 percent.

7. What is the cost of 40 boards 12 inches wide and 16 ft. long at $.20 per inch?

8. Find a bank discount on $300 for 90 days (no grace) at 10 percent.

9. What is the cost of a square farm at $15 per acre, the distance around which is 640 rods?

10. Write a bank check, a promissory note, and a receipt.

U.S. History (Time, 45 minutes)

1. Give the epochs into which U.S. History is divided.

2. Give an account of the discovery of America by Columbus.

3. Relate the causes and results of the Revolutionary War.

4. Show the territorial growth of the United States.

5. Tell what you can of the history of Kansas.

6. Describe three of the most prominent battles of the Rebellion.

7. Who were the following: Morse, Whitney, Fulton, Bell, Lincoln, Penn, and Howe?

8. Name events connected with the following dates: 1607, 1620, 1800, 1849, and 1865?

Orthography (Time, 1 hour)

1. What is meant by the following: Alphabet, phonetic orthography, etymology, syllabication?

2. What are elementary sounds? How classified?

3. What are the following, and give examples of each: Trigraph, subvocals, diphthong, cognate letters, linguals?

4. Give four substitutes for caret 'u'.

5. Give two rules for spelling words with final 'e'. Name two exceptions under each rule.

6. Give two uses of silent letters in spelling. Illustrate each.

7. Define the following prefixes, and use in connection with a word: Bi, dis, mis, pre, semi, post, non, inter, mono, super.

8. Mark diacritically and divide into syllables the following and name the sign that indicates the sound: card, ball, mercy, sir, odd, cell, rise, blood, fare, last.

9. Use the following correctly in sentences, cite, site, sight, fane, fain, feign, vane, vain, vein, raze, raise, rays.

10. Write 10 words frequently mispronounced and indicate pronunciation by use of diacritical marks and by syllabication.

Geography (Time, 1 hour)

1. What is climate? Upon what does climate depend?

2. How do you account for the extremes of climate in Kansas?

3. Of what use are rivers? Of what use is the ocean?

4. Describe the mountains of N.A.

5. Name and describe the following: Monrovia, Odessa, Denver, Manitoba, Hecla, Yu Aspinwall and Orinoco.

6. Name and locate the principal trade centers of the U.S.

7. Name all the republics of Europe and give capital of each.

8. Why is the Atlantic Coast colder than the Pacific in the same latitude?

9. Describe the process by which the water of the ocean returns to the sources of rivers.

10. Describe the movements of the earth. Give inclination of the earth.

The best way to cut the cost and improve the quality of education is to get government out of it. The schools could be owned by individuals, associations, or corporations and operated for profit or not-for-profit.

With government backing off and tax rates reduced, prosperous people would take interest in central-city schools because those are the most in need. The prosperous would pay some of the tuition, just as some wealthy individuals are doing now. They would probably compete as to whose name would be placed in a new gym or new classroom.

To cut the cost of education, especially at the lower levels, teachers would teach older children, and the older students would teach the younger ones.

In the old days, relatively few people went to college. Those who did became doctors, scientists, researchers, lawyers, executives, financiers, and such. Having the capabilities to do so, they earned high income. Contemporary social scientists figure that if government just arranged for more people to go to college, they would enjoy higher income. Whoops, they forgot about the capabilities. As a result, the academic credentials of millions of college students have been too low. They've switched to easier courses or just dropped out, feeling like failures. If they had obtained jobs after high school, they would have earned income right away, acquired skills, and developed confidence.

Colleges and universities have become cesspools of socialism. With a significant portion of their income derived from government, they have not only adopted government's dreadful ideas, they've also helped create them. They want most social and economic problems to be solved by a monolithic government. Guess who stands ready to advise the government along the way. Why, the professors, of course.

CHAPTER 10

ENDANGERED SPECIES

HUMAN BEINGS ARE AN ENDANGERED species, for several reasons:

- To sustain the population, the average woman must have 2.1 children. This means that quite a few women must have 3 children. In prosperous nations, not enough do. Unlike on family farms, children are usually not needed to enhance the family's income. In prosperous, urban life, children get in the way and cost a bundle.

- The pill makes it all too easy to avoid having children.

- Many parents stop at two children because they're required to use huge car seats for their children, and only two such seats fit in the rear seats of most cars.[25] Funny how often government laws and regulations have unexpected negative consequences. If government were much reduced, car-seat requirements for children would probably disappear. If other measures chosen by individual parents are not taken, children might be hurt in accidents more than they are now. But the chances for the survival of humanity would be improved. A society that accepts modest imperfection is a healthier society in the long run. The time horizon of government doesn't extend much beyond the next election.

- Government creates no wealth; it consumes wealth and impedes

---

25. Washington Examiner, October 13, 2020.

the creation of wealth by others. As government has grown to 40 percent of the gross domestic product (GDP), the financial pressure on people outside of government causes families to cut down on the number of children. Indeed, the growth of government throughout the world makes the prospects for the human species ever more ominous.

- Ubiquitous plastics contain toxins that scientists believe are causing sperm counts to drop by about 1 percent a year.

Back in 1960, India's fertility rate was 5.9. Now it's 2.0. The U.S. 1.7. Russia 1.5. China 1.2. South Korea a horrific 0.8. The people of many nations are on the road to extinction. The African people still have fertility rates well above 3.1. But they're striving to become prosperous. With their big governments, they will probably cause their fertility rates to drop.

Our successors, the robots, might put human survivors in zoos. Little robots would enjoy feeding us Twinkies.

CENSUS BUREAU

A *Wall Street Journal* column on September 20, 2022, entitled, "What the Child Poverty Rate is Missing," was written by Phil Gramm, former U.S. Senator from Texas, and John Early, formally Assistant Commissioner of the Bureau of Labor Statistics. They explain that, in calculating the 2021 poverty level of children, the Census Bureau failed to take into account food stamps, health insurance subsidies, rent subsidies, energy subsidies, refundable tax credits, Medicare, and over one hundred other federal, state, and local transfer programs, all of which increased the income of families with low earned income. If the subsidies had been counted, the child poverty rate would have been only 3.2 percent. The poverty rate reported for 2021 was 15.3 percent. Omitting the subsidies enables the administration to say to Congress, "Pity the poor children (sob). We simply must spend more."

GEORGE FLOYD'S ULTIMATE KILLER

The Minneapolis Police Department had received several complaints about the excessive use of force by Derek Chauvin, a member of the department. Because of pressure from the Police Union, the Minneapolis Police Chief had no authority to fire Chauvin or even reassign him. To enhance their personal wealth, union leaders endeavor to retain as many members as possible. If Chauvin had been fired, he would not have killed George Floyd, of course. Floyd's death, therefore, was ultimately caused by the union.

Unions are rich and largely independent. The public unions have "captured" the operating machinery of government. Elected officials, supervisory officials, police chiefs, school principals – all are relatively powerless in comparison. In addition, worker unions put employers on the defensive and increase hostility in the workplace. The wages of union members are unnaturally high, raising everyone's costs. The poor, who spend most of their income on living expenses and are not union members are especially affected. The excessive power and wealth of unions stem from the federal laws which empower them. Those laws should be repealed. Unions have run amok. They are among the highest contributors of campaign gifts to legislators. Without the federal laws that support them, they would not exist in their present form.[26]

Government should recuse itself from all interactions between employers and employees. Employees could still form unions, but they should be supported by private-sector rules, not government laws.

THE GREAT RESET

The 2030 Agenda of the World Economic Forum and the United Nation calls for the nations of the world to set up a command economy. They've signed strategic agreements with world powers and hundreds of non-

26. Philip K. Howard, "The New Nobility," Washington Examiner, September 19, 2023.

SHRINK GOVERNMENT: IT'S TOO BIG!

government organizations. The global governing power expects to fulfill a utopian vision of the world, with no poverty and no discrimination. It expects to reverse climate change by wiping out most fossil fuels. It expects to provide universal health and reproductive care, inflation control, equal distribution of food, digital IDs, and a universal living wage. It'll be a new world order with unelected officials controlling a command economy imposed on the entire world. This is world-wide communism. The United States signed up for it because . . . Gosh, I wonder why the United States signed up for it. Doesn't the government realize it would be required to relinquish its powers to an international dictatorship?

Take heed of worldwide communism. The means of production may or may not be owned by the government, but most prices would indeed be set by the government. Not just the prices of retail products, either. The components of products also have long supply lines. Each time items pass from one owner to another, there's a transaction with a price – a transaction that benefits both sides. With free-market capitalism, each price reflects actual supply and demand conditions right there and then. For the world economy, there are probably billions of transactions every day. No matter how capable the computers are, no command economy can accumulate the information contained in all those prices. The correct information cannot be obtained *except* by free-market pricing. The Great Reset is guaranteed to fail, causing misery for everyone other than the elite and those in government, but especially for the poor.

Thomas Sowell wrote, "The first rule of economics is that there's an infinite number of desires chasing a finite number of goods, services, and resources. The first rule of politics is to ignore the first rule of economics." Since the leaders of the Great Reset have not absorbed this truth, the effort will be a spectacular failure. The people who suffer most will be the poor.

In 1918, the Soviet Union created a department to set prices. Members of the department had no idea where to begin. Ah-*ha*, they acquired Sears Roebuck Catalogues, which were wonderful examples of capitalism. These gave the bureaucrats some idea of relative values. This helped, but eventually the Soviet Union failed anyway.

BRING DOWN THE RICH

Five of the seven U.S. counties with the highest median income are suburbs of Washington DC, where many bureaucrats live, not to mention lobbyists and politicians. Including benefits, federal bureaucrats are paid about 70 percent more than people with equivalent jobs in the private sector, and they're rarely fired. The rules and regulations they impose do hidden, long-term harm, and the people hurt most are the poor. Reducing the size of the federal government would save the nation considerable cost and trouble. It would also convert Washington, DC, into an average urban area, not one of the nation's richest.

GIVE THE CIVIL SERVICE THE HEAVE-HO

America's U.S. founders were all too familiar with the excessive power of European monarchs serving as executives, legislatures, and judiciaries. The founders wisely spread the powers among three separate government branches. A few decades ago, Congress gave federal bureaucrats the power to serve as an alternate executive, legislature, and judiciary, the very problem the founders sought to avoid. Fortunately, the Supreme Court of 2022 began to reverse the error.

The best way to prevent federal bureaucrats from serving as an alternate legislature, executive, and judiciary is to abolish the Civil Service and return to the former spoils system, whereby presidents can hire and fire whomever they like, whenever they like. With the spoils system, people paid for the privilege of serving, making the spoils system corrupt. But the corruption of the Civil Service is far more damaging. From behind the scenes, the bureaucrats lobby, often successfully, to enlarge the size and intrusiveness of government. This has hurt everyone – well, everyone except the bureaucrats. If the federal government and the amount of money it handles were much reduced, there would be less to be corrupt about.

When I suggested to a friend that we should deep-six the Civil Service system and return to the spoils system, he responded, "We can't go backwards."

Ha! We've *been* going backwards for over a century. The federal government has become bigger and bigger. As a result, the nation has become more and more dysfunctional.

Hundreds of thousands of government bureaucrats – honest, capable, hard-working people – should be required to leave government. They believe, incorrectly, that government is the best way to solve social and economic problems. Sorry, but in the private sector they would be more likely to *benefit* society for a change.

HAYWIRE IMMIGRATION

The United States has opened the immigration floodgate to people who come from big-government nations that are failing. The individuals want out of those countries. Most of them are probably unaware that big government is the cause of the problems they want to get away from. Few are familiar with the benefits of small government, free-market economics, and individual freedom. They're expected to vote for Democrats, who generally favor bigger government. The U.S. government, including the bureaucrats, is dominated by Democrats. They're the ones who have let in so many immigrants.

CHAPTER 11

EXECUTIVE COMPENSATION

DURING A RECENT EXCHANGE OF views, a liberal friend said she thought America's biggest problem is the greed of its corporate executives.

As discussed in some detail in the book, by far the most damaging greed is that of people in the public sector for more power.

For example, the federal government latched onto a respiratory disease (which federal funds provided by Dr. Anthony Fauci probably helped to create). The disease is highly contagious, but less deadly than the flu. The federal government's exaggerations generated tremendous fear among the people, which the government took advantage of to substantially increase its powers.

The government has created unjustified fears about global warming. It proposed substantial reductions in atmospheric CO_2 which would generate the need for heavy government involvement. The changes would be severe enough to damage modern civilization.

The government has accused Americans of racism. In the 1950s, when America really was racist, a Gallop pole showed that only 4 percent of the people supported interracial couples; now, 94 percent do. In advertisements in the 1950s, blacks were seldom seen, because whites would not have bought products that were recommended by blacks; now, advertisements are loaded with blacks. In movies, blacks appeared almost exclusively as servants; now, many movies have blacks in leading roles. Nevertheless, government and its sidekick, the media, have generated the mistaken belief that America continues to be racist and seek to involve themselves in every aspect of our lives to do away with it.

The following are the main reasons why the compensations of America's corporate executives have risen so high.

1. Corporate executives used to be concerned primarily with running the company. Now, executives not only manage the corporate affairs, but also deal with the government. Doing both requires remarkable individuals, causing their compensations to rise accordingly.

2. Markets that are free of government interference provide a check on excessive compensation. When executive pay is unreasonably high, the prices of the company's products are also high to provide the funds. Competing companies whose executive pay is reasonable can take business away from the other, because their prices are lower.

3. Companies today do not operate in a free-market environment because government is so deeply involved in their affairs. Government also tends to favor large corporations over small ones. Under these circumstances, the capacity of truly free markets to reduce corporate excesses is much less in operation.

SCIENCE HAS BECOME POLITICIZED

In the old days, scientists would develop a hypothesis, create an experiment, and determine that the hypothesis was wrong. This was progress; they'd learned that something was not true. Scientists were under no pressure to publish. They just went on to create and test another hypothesis. Thomas Edison tested some 2,000 materials before finding a filament that worked for light bulbs. More recently, government has flooded the universities with money, with the result that universities have trained too many scientists. This has changed the standards of success. No longer is it okay to be wrong. No longer can scientists get ahead without publishing. With the competition intense, they feel the need to study subjects in which they can be sure of being right, if only by a minuscule amount. They toe the government's line without considering opposing views. No longer just a search for truth, science has become politicized. [27]

GOVERNMENT'S PROPER DUTIES

Since about the middle of the Theodore Roosevelt Administration in 1905, the government sector of the United States has grown from 10 percent to about 40 percent of the GDP. Although people are far wealthier, the quality of life and morale for most people have declined, especially for those a on low income. American governments, especially the feds, are too big, too powerful, and too intrusive. The nation would be happier, more prosperous, and more equitable if the government sector were significantly reduced.

The feds are the most damaging part of the U.S. government, being the biggest and the furthest away from the people. The Feds should deal with home defense and immigration, with the Senate confirming the appointments of officials and federal judges. That's about it. On this basis, the federal legislature would be in session only a minority of the time.

The states should handle elections, as required by the Constitution. They should operate courts and have modest police power, keeping people from hurting others by force or fraud. The states should do away with the damaging policies mentioned in this book, and they should divest themselves of all educational institutions.

---

27. George Leef, "Higher Education is Complicity in the Politization of Science," The James G. Martin Center for Academic Renewal, August 23, 2022.

Local governments should exercise courts and most of the police power. An association of state and local police forces might coordinate their efforts nationally. Except for defense intelligence, and border protection, there should be little need for a federal police force because there would be few federal laws to enforce.

Of the three levels of government, local governments, being closest to the people, are the least damaging, with the exceptions being the dreadful, big-city governments controlled for decades by Democrats. The local governments should do away with the adverse policies mentioned in this book. They should not own or operate educational institutions.

The most active elements of government would be the courts, the police, the military, and the border police. Under these conditions, the government sector of the United States would be reduced from the current 40 percent of the GDP to 5 percent or less. Government would regulate nothing. The private sector would develop regulations where necessary, perhaps backed by the courts. The longer people live without government interference, the more they would identify with the entire society, not just their own particular circumstances.

Monies received by the courts in payment of fines should not be retained as large and permanent cash reserves. After covering their expenses, the courts should turn over these funds to administrators so that the tax rates may be reduced.

Government payments to some groups and not to others arouse resentment. People respond by trying to beat the government's system, which promotes selfishness. If government is greatly reduced, people would take responsibility, not only for their own actions, but also for the entire society. Less government means more selflessness. The most selfish part of our society is government, which wants to get bigger and more powerful regardless of whether this helps everyone else or not.

All taxes should be charged at rates that are flat and very low.

The earth has likely been infused with poisons, left over from the pell-mell technological growth of recent years. Technology would help clean up the poisons. But otherwise, we would probably be better off if the pace of technology slowed down, giving people time to adjust to the precipitous changes.

During past crises, such as America's wars, the Great Depression, and the 2008 Credit Crisis, government and the use of force expanded. After most of the crises passed, the government was knocked back, but unfortunately, not all the way back, enabling it to grow larger and larger over time. A major reversal is needed. It's time to reduce government all the way down to 5 percent or less of the GDP, where it belongs. Local governments outside the big cities would be affected least. The privatization of all schools would put a big dent in their affairs – a favorable change from the public's point of view. The federal government would be affected most. That gargantuan has become an absurdity.

Would everyone be content? Of course not. Every society feels it has problems. With government mostly out of the picture, there would be fewer serious problems. But given the complexity of the private sector, the solutions would be far more numerous and varied than they would be with government. Solutions that don't work would be reworked.

Government solutions result in bigger government and more use of force. These cause problems in addition to the ones the government first dealt with. Government then designs solutions for the new problems. The new solutions create even more problems. The result: a massive government and a multitude of problems, hurting the poor most.

Liberals assume that the supply of other peoples' money is inexhaustible. But the growth of government quenches the creation of wealth and makes other peoples' money less available. In the long run, government thus creates ever more needs but suppresses the availability of money to deal with them. America's current dysfunction would suggest that the long run has come home to roost.

Government consumes wealth, creates no wealth, and inhibits the creation of wealth. If it were greatly diminished, the income of most people would rise, and the gap between rich and poor would narrow.

It is time to place individual liberty at the forefront of our lives.

ABOUT THE AUTHOR

AS A FINANCIAL PLANNER, ARCHIE Richards was registered with the Securities and Exchange Commission as an Investment Advisor. From 2000 to 2007, he wrote weekly newspaper columns, "Richards on Money Matters," which were published in eleven papers nationwide, syndicated part of the time by Creators Syndicate. For McGraw-Hill, Mr. Richards wrote Understanding Exchange-Traded Funds. For Defiance Press & Publishing, Conroe, TX, he wrote America's Governments, Enemies of the Poor in 2020 and America's Bankruptcy Approaches in 2021. In 2022, the Mises Institute published his article, "A Renewed Libertarian America."

In the early 1970s, about the time radio talk programs were becoming popular, Archie was a stockbroker in Boston. One of the stations there had a fine afternoon talk show host. Archie called him every Wednesday at 2:00 p.m. to talk about money matters and economics. On one of his calls, the host said, "Wait a minute. I received a letter about you." He found the letter and read it on the air. It was from a student, who wrote, "Archie's explanations of economics are clearer than those of my professors at Harvard."

Visit www.ArchieRichards.com to help get this book, *Shrink Government: It's Too Big!,* into as many hands as possible, with the goal of influencing public policies for the better.

www.ingramcontent.com/pod-product-compliance
Lightning Source LLC
Chambersburg PA
CBHW072208270326
41930CB00011B/2579